DRILL

• • •

Fast & Furious
Book Promotion

Drill
Fast & Furious Book Promotion

Copyright © 2008 by Philip Davis

Requests to the Publisher for permission should be addressed to ATTN Philip Davis, ZDocs, Inc. 2989 South, 300 West, Salt Lake City, UT 84115 or emailed to phild@zdocsonline.com.

This book is dedicated to Dr. William Guillory,
a wise man who figured out how to
push me out of my comfort zone.

Acknowledgements

• • •

I've been waiting eight months to write this page. This book is dedicated to Bill (Dr. Guillory) because one day at breakfast he asked me if ZDocs (the self-publishing company I help run) can help authors sell books. I said no and he asked why not. That conversation two years ago created the spark inside me to look for innovative ways for authors to promote their books. About the same time Bill was pushing me to get off my butt, Shahar and Nashlah Boyanan of Buzz Booster, were opening my mind to the possibilities of the Internet. While we rarely agree on anything, I have immense respect for Shahar and Nashlah and recommend every entrepreneur to join their community at www.entrepreneur30.com. Much appreciation goes to the whole team at ZDocs who kept the lights on while I worked on this book and the website, www.authorsonthenet.com. Greg Glathar (VP Operations), Daphne Olsen (who designed the cover), Tatiana Haynes (who edited the book), Ben Bailey, Brenda Rogers and the whole crew. Special thanks goes to Wade Melton and Richard Lundquist at Elite Ops who helped conceive this idea over lunch (seems like all I do is eat). For Chris Conlan at Kaboodle Ventures who wrote the forward and helped me make a dent in the crowded blogosphere. And last, but not least, for my family who put up with a lot of late nights. My life's dream is that my daughters will one day not be surprised when I come home before 10 pm.

Forward

• • •

When Phil asked me to write this forward I wanted to come up with some clever lead-in anecdotes or quotations. I came up with these:

> "If a book was written, but nobody knew it was there, would it even be read at all?"

> "Teach a man to write and he'll type for six months; teach a man to promote and he'll be selling books for a lifetime."

After wasting about 10 hours combing through quotation sites, my copy of Bartlett's, the synonym finder, and even busting out my Ryrie Study Bible to use the index, I realized that I had just fallen victim to one of the basic tenets of Phil's *Drill* principles - work smarter, not harder.

Robert McCrum recently wrote in The Observer and I quote,

> "...according to the New York Times, there's a new book published in the United States every half an hour, and—wait for it—that's just fiction. R.R. Bowker, the company that compiles the Books in Print database in the USA, has calculated that no fewer than 175,000 new titles were published in 2003. That's one book roughly every 20 seconds."

Other studies have delivered results showing that 81% of Americans believe they should write a book, and over 6 million of them have already written the manuscripts. 81% of the U.S. Population translates to roughly 200 million, take out the kids and then cut it in half again, that's about 50 million books waiting to be written, or in some stage of development.

As technology continues to develop on the publishing side, becoming more and more affordable for the individual author, and the on and offline audiences expand as the information age leaves its infancy, the opportunity for an individual author or small publishing house to successfully promote themselves grows exponentially every year.

Phil, together with his partners, is creating a whole new industry of "self-promotion" for the author - a crucial element, and the missing link in taking your book from printing that first 100 copies you give out to friends and send to the monopolistic "big houses," to actually generating profitable sales. Until now the vast majority of promotional tools available for an individual author pretty much fell into the "$295 How to Write a Press Release" kit.

Phil's book provides hands on insight and resources that anyone, regardless of technical skills, marketing training or budget can immediately begin putting in place to generate buzz, awareness and sales for their work.

I've been privileged to get advance copies of the book and see it develop as a work in progress, and can honestly say that I'm moving from the group that "has a book in them" to the group "that's writing a book." I'm a marketing guy by trade, and my biggest obstacle, or excuse, was that I didn't know how to go about selling my book once I had it written.

If you're writing a screenplay, then the Bible is Syd Field's Screenplay, if you're serious about promoting your book and taking your authorship to the next level, Phil's book is destined to be the Bible of self-promotion for authors.

CHRISTOPHER CONLAN
President
The Blogmill

Contents

• • •

Prologue

. . .

Any author who keeps working is not a failure. He may not be a great writer, but if he applies the old-fashioned virtues of hard, constant labor, he'll eventually make some kind of career for himself as writer.
— Ray Bradbury

I once heard a story about a man who climbed a mountain to find buried treasure. When the man found the spot he believed the treasure to be buried, he began to dig. He dug night and day for years. He dug fast and he dug furiously, changing his digging methods to improve his efficiency and using new types of shovels to help him cut through the ever-changing ground. The man dug with passion and energy but as the days wore on, his optimism began to wane. And then one early morning, he woke up and decided he had done enough digging. So he loaded his broken shovels into his tiny wheelbarrow and went home.

A few days later, a goat fell into the massive hole the man had dug. When the goat herder came by to save his goat, he looked at the hole and wondered why someone had spent so much time digging in this particular spot. The goat herder climbed down the hole and sat for a while, pondering its mystery. At last he concluded that if someone had spent so much time and effort digging in this particular spot, there must be something of great value buried in the dirt.

The goat herder carried his goat out of the hole and then went back down with a stick. After digging a few minutes, his stick hit something hard and metallic. He bent down and brushed the last of the dirt away. The goat herder, with a few digs of his stick, had found the treasure the other man had worked so hard to find but had given up at the very moment success was at hand.

What Ray Bradbury said about working hard at your writing applies equally well to the amount of effort you will need to put forth to promote and sell your book. Using the Internet to sell books allows you to work fast and furiously and authors who keep at their task have a greater chance today of selling books than ever before.

Introduction

• • •

The Author's Mindset

DRILL is about promoting books online and when you work online the pace is certainly fast and furious. At ZDocs, the self-publishing company I own, we have been using Google adwords, a pay-per-click advertising method, for several years to find authors who need to print books. Our advertising was working great; so great that I was working with 40 authors and felt I couldn't take on another client. I was driving home one night at 9:30 pm wondering what I needed to do and thought, 'what if I point my Google ads to my corporate website instead of to my book website?' I got off the freeway and went to the closest Wi-Fi enabled coffee shop I could find. I turned on my laptop and 30 minutes later, I had made the change.

The next morning, almost 15 hours after making the change to my Google ads, I had a half million-dollar account asking me for a bid. I gave the company the bid. Two days later, I was meeting with the client and two weeks after that meeting we began publishing their seminar kits. Later, I wondered to myself what would have happened if I hadn't turned my truck around and changed my Google ads just minutes after I had had the idea. ZDocs might no longer be in business and I might be busy doing job interviews instead of helping people print and promote books.

I am not a Google ad expert. I am not a computer programmer. I am not a Search Engine Optimization expert. I do not know HTML or ASP or PHP. And yet, I have set up two websites and two blog sites virtually on my own and I have run my own pay-per-click campaigns and have had great success with them.

The point I am making is that the Internet is no longer a mysterious tool that only computer geeks know how to use. The

Internet is a tool anyone can use. Once you begin using some of the tools introduced in this book, you will be empowered to do what I did for my business. You can wake up one morning with an idea and within minutes implement that idea. The pace is fast and furious.

In addition to the concept of moving fast and working at a furious pace, is the concept of drilling as long as it takes to reach your goals. While we found our "mega" customer 15 hours after changing our Google ads, it really took us over a year to find that customer because that is how long ZDocs had been running its pay-per-click campaign. What if we had run our campaign for a month and then stopped?

While results can come fast, in most cases, results take a while. I talk to people all the time who say they started a blog but stopped after several weeks. They say that no one was leaving comments or no one was sending bid requests or no one was buying their books. Dr. Bill Guillory, a good friend, client and author of many books has a great blog at www.where-to-now.com. After several months of blogging, Bill said that despite having over 3,000 unique visitors a month, no one was buying his books. But Bill kept 'digging in his hole' and a few weeks later he called me and said he just received an order for 80 books.

The purpose of this book is to help authors develop a systematic approach to promoting books online. Online book promotion is a new landscape for many authors and this landscape shifts like the Sahara sand dunes. Sure, there are a few rocks in this shifting landscape—Amazon comes to mind—but every day new and exciting tactics pop up that can help authors promote their books; Second Life, peer-to-peer book reviews, and Google books, are a few of the more recent tactics to make the headlines.

Authors today have so many ways to promote their books the endeavor can sometimes seem overwhelming. Also, with so many ways to promote online, many authors jump right into using tactics without thinking about what they want to achieve. When I first thought about using pay-per-click advertising—a tactic—I locked myself away in a hotel room for 10 days because I knew if we were going to advertise online, we had to have a plan and it was critical that we knew our target audience. Once we had our plan, we spent two months creating our website to appeal to our target audience and when we began our campaign it took three days before we received our first order. That's pretty fast and I'm convinced the reason we are having such good results with our online marketing is that we took some time on the front-end to make a plan.

Authors, like any entrepreneur, can realize greater rewards if they first create a plan. A good plan starts with developing realistic goals, researching who your customers are and inventing a strategy for your book. Completing these three steps first is critical to effectively implementing any tactic, online or offline.

DRILL was written for both published and self-published authors. In addition, the readers I envisioned for this book are authors who have little or no experience using the internet to promote books or authors who want to learn more effective ways to use the internet. The book will take you through the critical steps necessary to create an effective plan and will show you how the Internet can help you complete these steps quickly and efficiently. The steps of the *DRILL* system are:

1. **D**—Develop realistic goals

2. **R**—Research your market

3. **I**—Invent your strategy

4. **L**—Layout your tactics

5. **L**—Leverage your assets

Some readers will jump right to the tactical sections of this book. However, if you begin to take actions without knowing what results you want, you risk wasting resources. I admit that coming up with goals, doing market research and writing down your strategy is not exciting, but I encourage you to take some time to think your strategy through and you will see that performing the upfront planning is not all that painful or boring.

Because the tools you can use, both online and offline, are continually changing, I do not attempt to list them all. Another reason I do not list every tactic is that I believe in the concept of "less is more." For example, I take about one page to discuss online book reviews. This page will take you about 5 minutes to read, but effectively implementing this tactic may take you a month. If I were to list 80 tactics in this book, most authors would be overwhelmed.

An important concept in *DRILL* is that each book requires a unique strategy for success and the best person to *invent* that strategy is the author. I am personally wary of "proven success strategies" for books. A strategy that worked for one author may not work for another author. If 4 million authors plan to sell books this year, these 4 million authors will need to create 4 million unique strategies to promote their books. The *DRILL* system is designed to help authors create their own unique strategy to sell *their* book.

While creating a unique system is vital to every book's success, most authors will spend most of their time and money on tactics. Deciding which tactics to use is important and complicated. To aid authors in making their decisions, we have created an online community called Authors On The Net (www.authorsonthenet.com) This website offers instructional videos on how to create a blog site, the contents of this book, hundreds of articles on book promotion, a connected blog community, blog creation services, Blog SEO services and many other resources for authors. You can access our system by subscribing to our website at www.authorsonthenet.com.

As a member of Authors On The Net, authors will have access to details on how to effectively implement online tactics and we will be constantly updating authors on new opportunities for book promotion. For example, I do not discuss the social networking community *Second Life* in this book, but we will have information on the Authors On The Net website that covers this service in detail. We will also include helpful hints like when you leave a comment on a blog you need to include the http:// before your web address. Including all this information in this book would require thousands of pages and take readers away from the important message of *DRILL*, which is to create an overall strategy for promoting books.

The Author's Mindset

Successful people work from a success-oriented mindset. A mindset is an attitude and refers to how we approach tasks. The author's mindset can be described as follows:

I Am Focused, I Am Independent,
I Am Innovative, I Am Determined

The following section describes each of these attitudes.

I Am Focused

My dog Koko is the most focused "person" I know. Koko is a chocolate Labrador retriever. Labs are designed to retrieve things. That's what they do. And Koko is great at what she does. Sometimes we go downstairs where there isn't anything she can break and I'll throw a tennis ball across the room. No matter where that ball ends up, Koko finds a way to get it. If the ball rolls under a couch, Koko will lay in front of the couch and stick her snout in as far as she can and try to dig it out with her front legs and if she can't reach it she'll start to whine and bark until she gets me to come and get it for her. I've never met anyone more determined and focused than Koko when she is in her retrieving mode. Authors need to be this focused if they are going to reach their goals.

Some authors I've worked with have described themselves as "scatterbrains," or, using the more popular term these days, ADD—Attention Deficit Disorder. This term is overused and misused. ADD is a term authors must scratch from their vocabulary.

I Am Independent

I love Home Depot's tag line, "You can do it; We can help." When an author asks me how our services work at ZDocs, I usually say we're like home depot in that our job is to provide you the tools so you can do your job. Even if a mainstream publisher such as Random House picks up your book, you will still need to promote it yourself. The concepts and tools in this book and the accompanying kit are for all authors who need to promote themselves, not just self-publishing authors.

Writing, publishing and promoting a book are not democratic endeavors. While it is great getting feedback from people like editors, designers, friends and colleagues, at the end of all the discussions, a decision still needs to be made. You, the author, must make that decision. Authors are fiercely independent.

I Am Innovative

This mindset relates to learning quickly and implementing what you learn at a furious pace. Good innovators are people who are not afraid of new ideas and when they find an idea that applies to them, they internalize that idea very quickly.

I go to breakfast once a week with the wisest man I know, Dr. William Guillory, CEO of Innovations International. Bill told me one day that truth is what we individually experience. We can learn from other people's experiences, but until we take action ourselves and create our own experiences, we will not know truth.

In my definition, this is what an innovator does. He or she learns new concepts and then quickly internalizes those concepts by putting them into action to create their own experiences, or in other words, their own truth.

I understand that we all learn differently. Some of us like to have a complete understanding of something before we go out and implement what we've learned. Others, like me, like to work at a furious pace and learn along the way. When you start to work on the Internet, this mindset of working furiously and learning along the way is a good mindset to have. That's why at AuthorsOnTheNet.com, we set out to build a learning system using Screen Capture software instead of just writing a standalone book with lots of examples of how other people have been successful.

Your experience is yours and yours alone. The purpose of this book is to give you ideas on how to create a system for selling your book, but when you achieve your success that success is yours and no one can define what that success will look like or feel like except you.

I Am Determined

Successful people dig until they find their treasure. They do not give up just inches away from success. Woody Allen once said, *"Eighty percent of success is showing up."* While this book discusses how to go about "showing up," finding the buried treasure lies in discovering the other 20%. The way I express this concept is:

> *If 80% of success is showing up, then 20% of success is digging until you reach your goals.*

In the early days of ZDocs, we hit a point when my accounting mind was telling me the smart thing to do would be to shut down. But I had recently read Richard Branson's book, *Losing My Virginity*, and one of the main points I took away from his 500 plus page autobiography was his concept of a turning point. Mr. Branson said that every time he was faced with a difficulty, such as running out of cash, he always chose to plunge ahead and grow rather than to contract or shut down.

When my partner and I met to discuss the decision of shutting down, she didn't want to close. But it wasn't her house being mortgaged to stay afloat, it was mine so I was feeling less enthusiastic about keeping the company alive. As we talked, we realized that we had just landed some really good accounts and we could both see that things were turning around. So I took Richard Branson's advice and mortgaged the house and four years later we are still alive and kicking.

However, at that moment when cash was tight, I was the man standing on the mountain digging a huge hole and at the point of going home. Thanks to my partner and to Richard Branson's book, I decided to keep digging. More than any other idea or tactic you might learn in this book, is the concept of grim determination and sometimes our determination is the very tool we need to find our buried treasure.

1
The DRILL System

• • •

*Success comes to a writer, as a rule, so gradually that it is
always something of a shock to him to look back and realize
the heights to which he has climbed.*
– **P. G. WODEHOUSE**

To explain the system for promoting books, I came up with
the acronym DRILL. I like this acronym for three reasons. One, it
goes well with the metaphor of this book, which is drilling fast
and furiously until you find your treasure. Two, a good acronym
helps people remember what the system is about, and, three, finding readers requires authors to "drill" deeply to find their target
audience.

Let's say you have a book on how to teach gorillas to communicate using sign language. You know your book will never be a
New York Time's bestseller because only a handful of people in
the world have any interest in teaching gorillas how to sign. But
after you've researched your market, you think there might be
10,000 people in the world interested in your topic. Most chances
are that a large publishing house won't publish you and bookstores won't want to devote their shelf space to you. But most of
your potential readers are well-educated people and they use the
Internet. You can find a percentage of your readers by drilling
into the Internet. The DRILL system is designed to help you find
those readers.

Once again, here is what the acronym DRILL stands for:

D—Develop realistic goals

R—Research your market

I—Invent your Strategy

L—Layout your tactical plan

L—Leverage your assets

Although you might think having a goal, a strategy and a tactical plan makes common sense (and I would agree with you), do you know how many authors have walked into my office with a strategic plan? *Zero.* Some authors have pretty good ideas about how they will sell their books, but not one author has been able to show me a detailed plan.

D—Develop realistic goals

The first part of the DRILL system is to develop realistic goals, or better yet, develop "One" realistic goal. The more you can focus, the better. Knowing what your goal should be takes a little thinking, and before you can create the right goal for your book you need to know what kind of book you have, what market need your book answers and the size of your target audience.

Not all authors have the goal of being a New York Times best seller or living the rest of their lives on royalties from their book sales. Some authors want to leave their stories behind for their children, others just want to get their first book published, and some want to create additional revenue to their consulting business. Your particular goal might be one of these or something entirely different.

To simplify the process of deciding on an appropriate goal for a particular book, I like to put books into two main categories. These categories are:

1. **Cultural Books**

2. **Commercial Books**

A Cultural Book is a family history, a memoir, a cook book, a collection of poems, a scrapbook, a children's book or some other book that has significant personal and family value, but probably little commercial value. The Cultural author seeks to preserve his or her heritage, or that of a community or club in the form of a professionally printed book.

A Commercial Book, on the other hand, is written with the intent to sell as many copies as possible. These books include novels, how-to books, business books, memoirs of famous people and so forth. Authors write these books with the intent of making money.

Before continuing, I should mention that some cultural books become commercial books and sometimes as a total surprise to the author. To see a great example of such a writer, go to http://www.richardpaulevans.com/biography.html to read Richard Paul Evans story, a very successful author who began by writing a story for his daughters and then one day decided to self-publish 20 copies to give to friends. Eventually his book, *The Christmas Box*, sold over 8 million copies and Mr. Evans is now a huge commercial author with several best sellers.

If you define your book as a Cultural book your goal will most likely be to print a small number of books for your family and friends and maybe for some local community centers and libraries. Your main focus will be on the manufacturing of your book, what type of paper to use, what kind of binding, etc. You will want to find a printing company that can produce the type of book you want in a cost-effective way. For most Cultural authors, creating an extensive promotional plan is not necessary. However, depending on the type of book you have, you may still want to put your book on Amazon and you may want to create a blog and maybe give your book some exposure without spending a lot of money. If so, the *DRILL* system can still be beneficial to you.

For example, we have several authors who are selling their Cultural books on Amazon, at local bookstores and by local word-of-mouth. Irv Cohen sells his nostalgic poetry books on Amazon and in retirement homes. Gary Kimball has two books about Park City, Utah and through some local media has sold several hundred copies of his books. Michelle Huggins sold all 100 copies of her hardbound poetry book at a single book signing in a local bookstore.

If you think you have a Cultural book that might have even a small niche market, then your goal might be to produce a hundred books and test the market. If that initial launch goes well, then you might create a new goal to sell 500 books and choose some grass roots ways to promote your book.

While I think Cultural authors might find the concepts and tools in this book useful, our primary target audience for *DRILL* is Commercial authors. One commercial author's goal might be to write a best selling novel or business book. Another author's goal might be to write a book to sell as part of his or her coaching business. Another author's goal might be to get his or her first book published, to gain credibility in the publishing world and open doors for future books that might *then* become best sellers.

The point is that not all authors have the same goal and only you—an independent author—can decide the best goal for you. Deciding on your goal will define the best approach to take to achieve your goal. For example, if your goal is to be a New York Times best selling mystery novelist, then the best strategy is selling your book to a mainstream publisher who specializes in publishing mystery novels. Your tactical plan will focus on how to get your manuscrj3\ sold.#4Èf a Commercial author asks me to help them define a realistic goal for their book, I generally recommend setting a goal to sell 5,000 copies. The average number of books sold in bookstores is 5,000 so a goal to sell 5,000 copies is both aggressive and conservative. This 5,000 number serves several purposes:

1. By focusing on selling 5,000 copies, you will see the value in printing in short-runs until your volumes begin to increase. Printing in short-runs helps you minimize risk by not tying up your cash in inventory.

2. Self-publishing is generally not the best approach if you want to sell your book to a mainstream publisher, but self-publishing can be beneficial if you can demonstrate to a

publisher that you have sold 5,000 copies through self-promoting efforts. Publishers like to invest in books that will be successful.

3. If you can sell 5,000 copies then you will make a profit from your book. You won't be financially independent for the rest of your life, but you will not have lost money either.

There are no hard and fast rules in the publishing game. I said above that if you're a novelist, you should focus on getting published because finding a publisher who specializes in your type of book is the intelligent approach. But JRR Tolkien, the author of *The Lord of the Rings* and *The Hobbit*, self-published. Richard Paul Evans self-published. James Redfield, author of *The Celestine Prophesy*, self-published. While the "rule" may be to find a publisher if you have a work of fiction, often, breaking that rule is the best choice you can make. For some books, self-publishing may be the only choice.

It takes, on average, 18 months to sell your manuscript to a mainstream publisher. That's a pretty big investment in time, or in other words, that's a pretty big hole to dig. But if your goal is to get published, then your strategy and your tactical plan should be built to achieve that goal. For example, you'll want to learn all about writing query letters and finding agents. Publishers want you to submit a query letter and many publishers won't look at anything unless it comes from a literary agent they know and trust. If your plan is to get published, then one of the best places to start is to buy a copy of the Writer's Market manual or to subscribe to their website, www.writersmarket.com.

The Writer's Market manual will tell you exactly how to submit your manuscript to publishers or literary agents who might be interested in your book. Yes, it will take a lot of digging until you sell your manuscript and after all that digging there is no guarantee you will find your treasure. But if your goal is to get published then you should exert all your effort to achieve it.

I'll explain what I mean by relating a story I read about Stephen King in his book *On Writing*, a book I recommend all authors read. In his book, Mr. King says that when he was getting started he would write stories and submit them for publication and each time he would get a pink rejection letter. He said he pinned each of these rejection letters on a nail in his room. He said he collected quite a number of these rejection slips and then one day he got a rejection slip back with a comment written on it. Mr. King said that when he saw that comment, he knew he would become a published writer.

I'm a big fan of Stephen King and I think he is a master of his craft. But success did not come easy for Stephen King. He dug and dug at his hole until he found his treasure. He did not give up a foot away from hitting pay dirt but rather he kept digging and while he was busy "digging" he was becoming a better writer. I believe that Stephen King is the writer he is because success did not come easy.

But let's get back to the point and the point is that your strategy and your tactical plan are derived by the goal you have for yourself and your book. Stephen King's goal was to make a living by writing. His goal wasn't to make his first story a New York Times best seller, but rather, his goal was to write and write and write until he became a best-selling author.

What is *YOUR* goal? Take a moment and write your goal on the opposite page. Be honest with yourself and be creative. In today's world, you do not need to be on the New York Times bestseller list to be successful. Also, look at where you are in your writing career. Are you an unknown author? If so, your chances of getting published are even harder. Maybe your goal should be to simply get something you've written published so you can begin to be noticed in the publishing world. Or maybe your goal is to become an expert in your field and a book is one step toward that goal. You are one of 4 million authors and you have a unique goal. What is that goal?

My Goal(s) for my writing career

Eyes Wide Open

When developing the goal you have as an author or the goal you have for your book, it is helpful to have a good understanding of the types of publishing available to you. I like to call this the *Eyes Wide Open* approach. This section discusses the three main ways to publish your book: Mainstream Publishing, Vanity or Subsidy Publishing and Self-Publishing.

The following is a comment I received on my blog site, www.howtopublishabookblog.com.

> Hello,
>
> Thank you for caring about the "little people" who have something worth saying and reading. As a writer, I've done a lot of research while trying to ascertain the best method to publish my literary projects.
>
> For many non-celebrity writers, using a large mainstream publisher is out of the question. If writers can create enough buzz about their book projects on their own, self-publishing is the best way to go. It also helps to know how to market and manage a business.
>
> Comment number 1 by: Manchild
> February 27th, 2007 at 5:28 pm

This author, codenamed Manchild, is one of at least 4 million other frustrated authors trying to get their books published. That's right, four million. And that is probably a conservative number. Each year about 175,000 titles are published with mainstream publishers. A mainstream publisher (MP) is a Random House or Ballantine type publisher. These publishers reject over 96% of the manuscripts presented to them. So if you run the numbers, you get a number close to $4.3 million authors seeking to get published each year.

With so many authors digging hard to find their target readers, many companies have entered the marketplace to service them. However, if you do not go into this greedy and manipulative marketplace with your *Eyes Wide Open*, you have a good chance of getting burned. And remember, the type of publishing you choose largely depends on the goal you have set for yourself.

Mainstream Publishing

Mainstream Publishing is the traditional way we think of publishing our books. This method is when a publisher like Scribner buys the rights to your book. Usually, a publisher will pay you an upfront sum of money and agree to pay you a royalty on every book that sells.

As I've said, an MP picks up only about 4% of authors and it takes on average 18 months from the time you send your query letters out to the time you sign a deal. But despite the difficulty, many authors who have written a book want to be picked up by an MP.

The reason you should try to sell your book to an MP is that going mainstream is the most cost-effective way for you to sell books. You will pay nothing to have your book edited, the cover designed, the books printed and distributed and most importantly, you will not pay for promoting your book. The publisher pays those expenses. That's why it's so hard to sell your book to a mainstream publisher. MPs are venture capitalists—make no mistake about it.

But here's an eye-opener: even if a MP picks you up and the MP is investing in your book, you will still be required to self-promote your book. That's why we do not consider the *DRILL* system to be just for self-publishing authors. All authors need to become effective self-promoters. Don't just take my word. Here's another blurb from my blogsite by Gloria Oliver, reprinted with her permission:

> "One of the BIG shocks after I finally got a clue and was able to get accepted by a publisher and got one of my works in print was a facet of the business I'd never imagined—I now had to push and SELL. Mind you, I was of the long-standing belief that a large majority of

writers were shy, reclusive people, who wrote books and then let the publisher take over as they went on and wrote more books. Something that sounded fabulous to my personality type.

Nothing could be farther from the truth.

Yes, once upon a time, publishers did take care of everything and writers only wrote. But in the last twenty years or so, the publishing industry has gone through a great upheaval. A lot of the old altruism is gone and the corporations have evolved to be run by accountants and marketing folks rather than nurturing editors. Publishers are now in the interest of actually making a PROFIT.

I don't blame them. We all want to make money. Unfortunately, however, this has affected the role of the writer and the expectations placed on them as to what they bring to the table, before, during, and after working on a manuscript.

So now, after going through the painstaking years to create your novel, beat it into shape, market it around, and finally (if the stars align just right) get a publisher, your work is only now truly beginning. For once your book is on the cusp of release, you must get yourself out there and sell yourself, your book, some might say your soul."

Gloria Oliver
Unveiling the Fantastic
http://www.gloriaoliver.com/

If your book is a success, the MP is positioned to make more money than the author. Many authors I talk to complain that the publisher made more money on the book than the author did. These authors are not factoring in all the risk the publisher put into the book. In my opinion, publishers need to compensate authors fairly, but the publishers deserve their profits because they are taking the bulk of the financial risk.

Another real-life story is that of Rebecca Wells, author of *The Divine Secrets of the Ya-Ya Sisterhood*. *"Divine Secrets"* sold 60,000 copies before its publisher decided to spend significant advertising dollars to promote the book. Ms. Wells spent hours upon hours promoting her book at book signings before a grass-roots movement created by word-of-mouth motivated the publisher to invest money to push the book.

As I've said, publishers are basically venture capitalists. Publishers not only invest in your book by paying you an advance, they also invest by paying all the costs associated with producing and promoting your book. And they do this without any guarantees your book will sell. That's why they like to go with an author who is already a known entity like Stephen King or President Bill Clinton or the serial killer on death row who's been in all the newspapers.

As you've probably guessed by now, I'm a huge Stephen King fan. I think he's a damn good storyteller and I've liked every story I've read of his except one. And with that one book, Mr. King's publisher may have had 1,000 other novels by other authors to choose from, but if you were in the business of making money, whom would you have gone with? Simply by putting Stephen King's name on the book virtually guaranteed the book to become a New York Times bestseller, even though the story may have been a complete loser compared to hundreds of other possible titles.

I have independent authors come in my office every week telling me they have a "great" book—a "blockbuster" book to use the term these authors generally use. And they might be right, but the cold, hard truth is that just having a great book is not going to get you published. You have to know how the game of publishing works.

As I've already mentioned, if your goal is to get picked up by a MP, I can't emphasize enough the importance of getting your hands on a copy of the Writer's Market handbook. The Writer's Market describes in detail how each publisher will accept manuscripts for consideration. Some publishers only work with literary agents so

Writer's Market explains how to contact literary agents and gives you their contact information.

If you think a MP will have interest in your book, then I say do your best to get picked up by a mainstream publisher. But brace yourself for all the rejection letters you may get, even if you do your homework and approach only those publishers who might be interested in your book.

One strategy I often recommend to our authors is to self-publish while they work on getting published. If you have the financial resources to self-publish and, more importantly, to self-promote, then I think this strategy has merit. If you go into the self-publishing game knowing that publishers will not be impressed unless you can show them significant sales (usually 5,000 copies) then I personally think that self-publishing while you are trying to get picked up by a MP is a good strategy.

An author once told me he sold 2.5 million books on his own and then finally a MP picked up his book and the MP sold another 500,000 copies. Mark Haroldson is an amazing self-publishing story; so amazing he actually did better than the publishing company. But the point still holds true that you can get picked up by a MP if you successfully self-publish.

The final point I'll make in this section about MPs is that MPs like to invest in known entities. Ninety-nine percent of authors I work with who have tried to get published tell me the rejection letters they received from publishers said that they—the publishing company—only work with "known" authors. Herein lies the catch 22 for new, unpublished authors. How do you become a "known" entity if no publisher is willing to give you that first crack at publishing?

DRILL is first and foremost built to help ALL authors (published and self-published) promote themselves and their book. That is our stated goal. The tools you will learn in this book are promotional tools that give you the chance of becoming a "known" entity. If no one knows your book exists, no one will buy it. The distinction between selling books and promoting books may be subtle, but understanding the difference is vital.

Vanity or Subsidy Publishing

Vanity publishing exists because the market of authors working hard to get published is large. But since only 175,000 authors will successfully get published, millions of other authors will seek alternative ways to get their books printed and sold.

Vanity/Subsidy publishing and self-publishing are close relatives and the differences can be hard for many authors to identify. Vanity or Subsidy publishing companies work in the grey area of publishing and one way you can determine if you are working with a Vanity press is if they are asking you to pay all the expenses to get your book published. That's why Vanity publishing is synonymous with Subsidy publishing. You, the author, are subsidizing the publishing of your book.

Another way to determine if you are working with a Vanity press is how the company handles the ISBN registration. If the company is going to own the ISBN and pay you a royalty on book sales, then I would encourage you to research the company by simply going online and finding out what other people who have used that company are saying about their experience. I would also encourage you to look hard at self-publishing because when you self-publish, you still pay all your own expenses, but you keep total control of your book and you keep all the profits.

The third way you can determine if you are working with a Vanity press is if they charge a package fee of say, $3,000 and in this package they provide you with 50 copies of your book and then they say the remaining money will be used for marketing. These packages sound very appealing, but again, do a simple Google search on the company and find out what people are saying about the company. In my opinion, if you are going to spend any money publishing your own book, you should get what you pay for.

For example, for about $1,300 you can get 250 printed copies of your book with just about any on-demand printer like ZDocs. If you pay $3,000 and get 50 books and if we assume each book costs $10.00 to produce, then where is the other $2,500 going?

You may find after reading this book that you can find more cost-effective ways to spend that $2.500.

To summarize, Vanity or Subsidy Publishers create the appearance of being your publisher, but you are going to pay all the expenses to print and market your book. When you begin looking for a place to publish your books, you will find companies like LuLu.com, Author House, Publish America and so forth. This book will cover a few of these companies, but the book that can help you decide which company to use is called *The Fine Print of Self-Publishing* by Mark Levine. You can buy a copy of his book at http://www.book-publishers-compared.com/

Another term often substituted for Vanity publishing is POD—printing on demand. I came across POD companies when I started working on the ZDocs marketing plan several years ago. Printing-On-Demand is what companies like Kinko's, Alphagraphics and ZDocs do, but somehow this term POD has been defined in the publishing industry as vanity printing, which is certainly different from what ZDocs, the company I own, does.

Here's another blurb from my blog site, www.howtopublishabookblog.com that will shed some light on the differences between Vanity/Subsidy/POD publishing and Self-Publishing:

> "In this entry, I'll be comparing Vanity or Subsidy publishing with Self-Publishing. There is quite a bit of bad press out there regarding Vanity publishing. It's not my place to criticize the Vanity press business model and therefore I will not be mentioning names in this article.
>
> My understanding of a Vanity press is these companies sell themselves as a publishing company to authors. As a publishing company, they own the ISBN number and share in the profits of book sales. As with self-publishing, an author pays all the costs when working with a vanity press, but in most cases the author has less control and does not receive all the profits of

the book. An author might choose vanity publishing over self-publishing with hopes the vanity press can help them sell more books.

Perhaps the best way to explain the differences between Vanity presses and Self-publishing companies is to create two comparative lists. So here they are:

Vanity Presses
1. The Author writes the book
2. The Vanity Publisher owns the ISBN number
3. The Author pays the Vanity Publisher to design the cover and the inside page
4. The Author pays the Vanity Publisher to edit the book
5. The Author pays the Vanity Publisher to print the book
6. The Author builds his/her own website or pays for someone else to do so
7. The Author and the Vanity Publisher jointly promotes the book
8. The Vanity publisher shares in the profit of the book

Self-publishing companies
1. The Author writes the book
2. The Author gets his/her own ISBN number
3. The Author designs the cover and the inside pages— or pays someone to do so
4. The Author pays someone to edit the book
5. The Author pays someone to print the book
6. The Author builds his/her own website or pays for someone else to do so
7. The Author does his/her own promotions
8. The Author takes home most of the profit

If you compare these two laundry lists above, you will begin to see why using a Vanity Publisher may not be a good choice. With both types of publishing, you, the author, are paying for everything—you are taking the entire up front risk. With Vanity or POD publishing, you are sharing the profits of your book with the publisher, a publisher who has taken little, if any, risk regarding your book.

With Vanity or POD publishers you will also find that you have less control, unless you use LuLu.com. I have authors share with me the difficulty they have experienced making changes to covers designed by the POD company they used. Authors are often told that the POD designers know more about cover designs than the author so just trust us. Most authors, who are fiercely independent, don't care for this approach.

Self-Publishing

Have you heard of any of the following?

- **Celestine Prophecy**, by James Redfield. The novel was self-published by the author in 1993 through Satori Publishers, which sold 100,000 copies. Redfield re-sold the rights to Warner in 1994. As of 2004, it has sold over 5 million copies in its Warner edition after well over 50 printings; world-wide, nearly 12 million copies in print in more than 40 languages.

- **Feed Me, I'm Yours**, by Vicki Lansky. This cookbook was self-published in 1975 by Meadowbrook Press, an imprint the author founded and continues to manage. In all, it has sold 3 million copies worldwide.

- **Invisible Life**, by E. Lynn Harris. This successful African-American novelist self-published his first book in 1991 and sold 10,000 copies. In 1994, Doubleday offered him a mass-market contract and went on to sell more than 500,000.

- **The Christmas Box**, by Richard Paul Evans. Evans originally conceived of this story as a gift for his family in 1992. He printed 20 copies at a Kinkos, and ultimately published and sold 250,000 paperbacks himself. In 1995, Simon & Schuster bought the rights and sold more than 7 million copies worldwide.

These authors all began by self-publishing, and yet you can find people all over the net telling you that self-publishing is the road "losers" travel. While I agree that self-publishing is not the best fit for all books, I do think that self-publishing is a great choice for many authors and the authors above are examples of people who have become great success stories by starting out self-publishing.

One of the key points to keep in mind when self-publishing is that when you self-publish you are running a business and when you run a business you run the show. Of the four authors above, the only one I have met personally is Richard Paul Evans and what I know of his story is that he didn't follow the normal publishing rules.

As his background was advertising, Mr. Evans took an aggressive approach when promoting his book, *The Christmas Box.* An urban legend in Salt Lake City, Utah is that Mr. Evans ran his book campaign like a political campaign. Another legend is that when he attended a book show in Las Vegas he acquired an empty seat of a New York Times best selling author who was supposed to be present but who never showed.

While I can't confirm either one of these urban legends, I can send you to http://www.richardpaulevans.com/biography.html, his website and you can read for yourself how Mr. Evans got started. And whether these "urban" legends are true or not, the stories do convey a message all self-publishing authors need to hear: to get noticed, you often have to do something unconventional.

When we work with authors at ZDocs, we emphasize that the author is in control. Here's a comment from Michelle Huggins, an author we worked with at ZDocs:

> "When you decide that you are serious about publishing a book, options seem limitless. There are so many

resources but there is a trade off. The more you give up by attempting to simplify the process, the more you lose control of your final product. It is after all sup-posed to be "self" publishing . . . In the space of less than twelve weeks we had the book completed and avail-able in local bookstores. The response was phenom-enal. My first "signing" *Confessions of an Angry Woman* sold out. There was a line out the door of the Spotted Frog Book Store. Chairs had been set up but it was standing room only. The local paper had done an ar-ticle about my book and mentioned the signing. There are so many things important to the success of any such endeavor, but when you go about it on your own, I feel a key to success is to never lose control of your book."

Another author we worked with, Larry Rigby, also took a very hands-on approach when publishing his first novel, *The Jäger Artist*. Larry is a successful businessman, so he quickly saw the advantage of starting his own publishing company. And like Michelle, he went to the paper store and picked out the exact paper he wanted, he found an artist to create his book cover and he oversaw the entire creation process.

The point of relating these two stories is to illustrate the dif-ference between self-publishing and mainstream publishing and vanity publishing. No one can tell you what is the right approach for you to take, but hopefully this book will help you make the right decision and give you the tools to promote yourself regard-less of which way you publish because regardless of how you publish, you will need to promote your book.

Self-publishing has several possible pay-offs. The first pay-off is the joy you'll feel when you see your book in print. Seeing your book in print is quite rewarding, so rewarding the Vanity presses are making millions each year helping authors print books. Make no mistake about it, seeing your book in print is very re-warding. In fact, every time an author's book comes off the binder

I feel this sense of pride although I'm just the printer, not the author. Seeing your intangible idea in the tangible form of a book is a great feeling.

The second great pay-off is that you are in control, as the stories of Michelle and Larry point out. While I liked working for Kinko's International and Flow International, my experiences with those two large companies cannot compare with the experiences I've had running my own small company. I'm working twice as hard for less money, but I'm enjoying every minute of it. Self-publishing authors will have this same pay-off.

The third pay-off is that you will make more money per each book sold than if you publish with a MP or if you use a Vanity Publisher. The numbers are pretty straightforward. If it costs you $5.00 to print your book and you sell your book for $15.00, then you net $10.00. You won't make $10.00 per book if you sell your book to a publisher and you probably won't make $10.00 per book if you use a Vanity press since you will share your profits with them.

But while you will make more money per book when you self-publish, whether you will actually *make money* is a function of your marketing plan. The next chapter will delve deeper into what a marketing plan is and how you can go about minimizing the inherent risk associated with self-publishing.

2
Research Your Market

• • •

Your stuff starts out being just for you... but then it goes out. Once you know what the story is and get it right—as right as you can, anyway—it belongs to anyone who wants to read it. Or criticize it.
– STEPHEN KING

Chapter One covered developing the right goal or goals for your book—the "D" in the DRILL system. While writing this book, I spent a lot of time reading blogs by many aspiring authors. One author, an aspiring novelist, wrote on her blog how she was contemplating self-publishing her second novel as trying to get her book sold to a mainstream publisher just about drove her crazy. As I read her blog, I felt she was giving up on her goal of becoming a published writer.

She also mentioned that after failing to sell her book to a mainstream publisher, she used a company to "self-publish" her book. I put self-publish in quotation marks because the company she used is, in my opinion, a Vanity press and not a true self-publishing company as I defined the service in Chapter One.

I mention this author's story to illustrate a couple of points. First of all, by reading her blog I sensed her confusion on how best to go about selling her book. The comment I left for her simply encouraged her to focus on her goal of getting published because with a novel, getting published is the best investment in both time and money. She may need to write 10 books before she reaches her goal, but getting published is the right goal for this author. If she keeps using Vanity presses, she will waste money and valuable time.

The second point I mentioned to this author is that if she decides to self-publish, then she needs to have the specific goal of selling 5,000 copies and to build a marketing plan to achieve that goal. While self-publishing is not the best method for her to reach her goal of getting published, self-publishing with a plan to sell 5,000 books is a plan that puts her in control. No one can sell your book like you can. No one will have the energy and passion for your book like you will. A true self-publishing plan is a plan that puts you in control of your book's success.

Regardless of which publishing road an author decides to go down, the author will need to self-promote his or her book. By now you should have a good idea what your goal is and what type of publishing will help you achieve your goal. The next step, the "R" in the DRILL system, is to research your market. As Stephen King said, you may have written your story—your book—for you, but eventually it's the readers who will "own it".

You may think that creating a marketing plan is boring stuff. I hope not because every expert in the publishing (and business) field will start off by helping you create a good marketing plan. Here's something I learned running my own company:

> The mark of a successful entrepreneur is someone willing
> to do the things they most dislike doing.

What does this mean? Here's what my experience taught me:

I like marketing and selling, but when we started ZDocs, I found myself doing a lot of accounting. As the owner of ZDocs, I should not have been doing so much accounting. We had a bookkeeper on staff, but she was also our primary customer service person and that role was more important to the company than the bookkeeping role was at the time. As we couldn't afford more staff, I had to step in and just do it. Once the business grew and cash flow improved, I started delegating as much of the accounting work as possible.

Now, many people, I should say, many authors love to create and to write. But do they—do you—like to sell? Maybe you do and maybe you don't, but the point is that it doesn't matter. Even if a mainstream publisher picks you up, you are going to be required to go to book signings and do interviews with the media. You may hate doing these things, but if you want to be successful, you will need to do them.

When you find yourself doing something you really don't like doing, think to yourself that the thing you hate doing most may be the one thing that will make you successful. And when you can afford to have someone better than you do that thing, then delegate as fast as possible. The key point here is finding someone better than you.

Your book will have a much better chance succeeding if you work from a good plan. The good news is that a marketing plan is not all that difficult or boring. In addition, as a member of Authors On The Net, you will have access to tools that help simplify creating your marketing plan.

My experience both with business owners and with authors is that if the planning process is time consuming or difficult, they simply won't do it. The underlying problem, however, is if the business owner or author does not see real value in creating a plan, he or she will not spend time planning. My intention is to both show the real value in planning and to give authors tools to help simplify the planning process.

Your marketing plan should have started before you wrote your first paragraph, but unfortunately, many authors I work with skip this step. It is common for professional writers to not write their book until they have identified who will want to read their book. Often, these writers will send off query letters to publishers before they write their book and they won't write the book until they have sold the idea first. These writers know they must have the right product for the market they are chasing.

I am passionate about the future of self-publishing. But for self-publishing authors to be successful, they need to make a product that a certain number of people have a demand for. You do not need to sell to a million people, but you do need a market large enough to justify spending so much of your time, energy and, of course, money.

Becoming a marketing guru is vital to your success as an author and in today's Internet-enabled world you have some incredible tools at your disposal to reach your target audience. But to reach this target audience, you need to know who they are, what they want and how to present your product to them.

Throughout this book, we will use one of our authors, Diana Derval, as a case study. You can find out all you need to know about Diana by going to her blog site at www.wait-marketing.com. Diana is the author of a book called, *Wait Marketing, Communicate at the right moment at the right place.* She first published her book in French, as her native language is French. She contacted ZDocs through our partner company Razorpages and I thought it would be interesting to work with Diana to get her book ready for the US market and then apply the *DRILL* system to create a strategy and tactical plan for her US launch.

Diana, Professor of marketing at the University of Wales MBA/Robert Kennedy College, wrote her book as part of her overall plan of becoming a world-renown marketing guru. One of the first discussions we held was what her goals were for her book. We decided on the following goals:

1. To sell **2,500** copies **6** months from the launch date (June 15th)

2. To have **her** book picked up by a major publisher in **her** field

3. To close 2 seminar clients each month

4. To close 2 speaking engagements each month

The process for coming up with these goals is described in more detail in Chapter Eight, Leveraging Your Tactics. Your goals drive your plan so having a clear picture of what you want to achieve is critical. The next step is to find out what your target audience looks like.

Your target audience determines every step you take with your book project. Your target audience helps you write your book, design the cover, choose your title, and of course, decide how to promote and sell your book.

Diana had a pretty good idea who she was writing her book for and this knowledge helped her decide on her title, *Wait Marketing*, which is a good title because it is short, direct and tells readers what the book is about. Her sub-title, *Communicate at the right moment at the right place*, is also appropriate and tells customers a little more about what to expect if they read her book. For non-fiction books, especially business related non-fiction books, the subtitle is often more important than the main title.

Knowing her target audience also helped Diana create a professional-looking cover. Here is what her cover looks like:

This cover is clean and professional. The picture is an attention grabber with a cute dog "waiting" with its owner. Covers are critical marketing tools. One recommendation I have is to require your designer to read your book before he or she designs the cover. Your designer should come to you with three to five choices and hopefully at least one of the designs will be right. You will know the right cover when you see it. If you don't like any of the designs, you may need a new designer  or you may need to get involved and give your designer ideas to work with. Be careful not to settle for a cover design you are not proud of because you will be the one out selling.

Diana wrote her book for Entrepreneurs, Academics, and Marketing Professionals. These groups represent a well-defined target audience, but through our discussions, Diana decided to narrow this target audience to large organizations with multiple operating units. A company such as Starbucks fits this target audience.

This target audience is very different than the target audience of, say, all marketing professors in the US—the academics of our society.

One day I received an email from an author who said her book is for everyone. That's the same thing as saying her book is for no one. Don't be afraid of focusing on one target customer. The internet tools you have at your disposal today will allow you to drill deep for your target customer and believe it or not, other people besides your target customers will buy your book. Although ZDocs does not advertise for business cards, we still get a lot of orders for business cards. You will reach customers outside of your target audience, but you cannot afford to go after all segments.

With this target audience in mind, Diana and I went to the Internet to find the most innovative companies who fit our target audience. We specifically wanted innovative companies because it will take forward-looking companies to become the early adopters of her concepts. Here is what we found:

The Top 50 innovative companies in the world

APPLE	Cupertino, CA USA
GOOGLE	Mountain View, CA USA
TOYOTA MOTOR	Toyota Japan
GENERAL ELECTRIC	Fairfield, CT USA
MICROSOFT	Redmond, WA USA
PROCTER & GAMBLE	Cincinnati, OH USA
3M	St. Paul, MN USA
WALT DISNEY CO.	Burbank, CA USA
IBM	Armonk, NY USA
SONY	Tokyo Japan
WAL-MART	Bentonville, AR USA
HONDA MOTOR	Tokyo Japan
NOKIA	Espoo Finland
STARBUCKS	Seattle, WA USA
TARGET	Minneapolis, MN USA
BMW	Munich Germany

SAMSUNG ELECTRONICS	Seoul South Korea
VIRGIN GROUP	London United Kingdom
INTEL	Santa Clara, CA USA
AMAZON.COM	Seattle, WA USA
BOEING	Chicago, IL USA
DELL	Round Rock, TX USA
GENENTECH	South San Francisco, CA USA
EBAY	San Jose, CA USA
CISCO SYSTEMS	San Jose, CA USA
MOTOROLA	Schaumburg, IL USA
SOUTHWEST AIRLINES	Dallas, TX USA
IDEO	Palo Alto, CA USA
IKEA	Helsingborg Sweden
DAIMLERCHRYSLER	Stuttgart Germany
HEWLETT-PACKARD	Palo Alto, CA USA
NIKE	Beaverton, OR USA
BP	London United Kingdom
RESEARCH IN MOTION	Waterloo Canada
AT&T	San Antonio, TX USA
CITIGROUP	New York, NY USA
VERIZON	New York, NY USA
ROYAL PHILIPS ELECTRONICS	Amsterdam The Netherlands
NINTENDO	Kyoto Japan
COSTCO WHOLESALE	Issaquah, WA USA
VOLKSWAGEN	Wolfsburg Germany
PFIZER	New York, NY USA
BEST BUY	Richfield, MN USA
JOHNSON & JOHNSON	New Brunswick, NJ USA
AMGEN	Thousand Oaks, CA USA
MERCK	Whitehouse Station, NJ USA
NEWS CORPORATION	New York, NY USA
MCDONALD'S	Oak Brook, IL USA
LG ELECTRONICS	Seoul South Korea
EXXONMOBIL	Irving, TX USA

From this list, it is interesting to see that Starbucks is the 14th company, which is a complete coincidence and validates our idea that large companies with multiple operating units are the target audience we should attack. This Google search took all of 3 minutes to conduct and coming up with our target audience took about 30 minutes total. Granted Diana is a marketing professional, but for most authors identifying a target audience does not take that much time or effort.

To illustrate this point, I will use a fictitious author named Sally. Let's say Sally has written a book to help elementary teachers teach gifted children. Sally's product is her book and she'll need to write her book with her audience in mind. She'll come up with a title and a cover design to appeal to her target audience. So who is her target audience?

Sally correctly identifies that elementary school teachers are her target audience. But what does that market look like? A one-minute Google search gives her quite a bit of insight.

Data from her Google search:

3.1 million elementary and middle school teachers in the US, of whom 79% are women.

From this one-line statement, Sally realizes that the bulk of her target audience will be women. She hadn't really thought about her market being mainly female as she was thinking of her market as one big bucket—elementary teachers.

Sally also finds a chart showing her a breakdown of teachers teaching other grade levels.

	Number	Percentage women
Preschool and kindergarten	442,000	98
Secondary	772,000	59
Postsecondary	1.1 million	46
Special education	175,000	87
Other teachers and instructors	562,000	67

The data above gives Sally some important insights. For example, it is clear that her product/book needs to be made with women in mind. This knowledge will help her when writing/ editing her book, coming up with the right title and designing the cover. Even though Sally wants all teachers to read her book, by focusing on the largest segment gives her book the best chance to succeed. In addition, just because her focus is on women teachers, it doesn't mean male teachers won't read her book. Actually, if she can sell effectively to women readers, these female teachers will most likely recommend their male counterparts read Sally's book.

Sally is right to focus on elementary teachers as that segment comprises the largest pool of potential readers, but the table above shows other segments she may want to keep in mind. For example, she sees an interesting segment of Special Education teachers and this gives her some ideas on some other possible sales channels and perhaps an interesting twist for some press releases.

In a matter of minutes, Sally has identified her primary target audience and some sub-segments. This information will help Sally in every aspect of her marketing plan, from creating and designing the product to deciding on the right price and deciding how best to promote her book. We could have narrowed her audience even further by identifying the age range of women teachers who are more likely to buy books and other demographic information. Your book may require this kind of detail. For example, are 40 year-old Hispanics your target audience? The more narrow your focus, the greater your chances of success in your initial marketing activities. You can always expand your audience as you grow, but more likely, other target audiences will find you and that is the best way to find your readers.

Before moving onto the next subject, pricing your book, I want to go back to an earlier comment. I said that coming up with a target audience does not take that much time or effort and I went on to give two examples of how we identified a target audience. The difficulty in deciding a target audience is not so much in the time it takes to research (which can be done at lightning speed with the internet), but rather the difficulty lies in making a decision. Deciding to focus on one group of readers is frightening.

But I know from experience that the more focused you are, the better your chances for success.

When we started ZDocs, we were a digital printer looking to print anything for anybody. For the first two years we struggled under this vision. Then one day we decided to focus on book publishing. It took us two months to reinvent ourselves and once we knew what customer we were serving, our business took off exponentially. We are in our 5th year at ZDocs and growing over 160% year-on-year. The single reason for our success can be traced back to making the decision to focus on authors and printing books. When I look back to the process of making that decision, it was a painful experience. Choosing one market to focus on scared the hell out of me. But what we learned was that the Internet gave us the ability to "*Drill*" down deep into this target audience. This same concept applies to authors selling books.

Take a few minutes now and write down on the following page the target audience that fits your book best. Feel free to do some simple research on the Internet to help you define your audience as narrowly as possible.

My Target Audience

Pricing

Authors often ask me how they should price their book. The answer is both simple and complicated. The simple answer is that the average paperback book sells for $14.95. The complicated answer is that you need to do a little research. The first two places to go are www.amazon.com and www.barnesandnoble.com. Look at similar titles and their prices.

Two other useful online sites for price research are www.aaabooksearch.com and www.123pricecheck.com. After searching online, the next step is go to "offline" bookstores and check the prices for books similar to yours. The reason I suggest to conduct your price search both online and offline is that online retailers tend to charge lower prices than bricks and mortar bookstores charge.

When you are doing your research, keep in mind that your price should be based on the market and not on what it cost you to print the books. Also keep in mind that the value of your book is the idea it conveys and not the paper it is printed on. This point is especially important when you are deciding on what to charge for your ebook. Many authors think they should charge a much lower price for ebooks because it doesn't cost anything to reproduce an ebook, but I disagree with this tactic unless it is part of an overall strategy.

For Sally's book, she may have to research books sold through a distributor that specializes on selling to school districts. Her book may need to be priced higher as she may be discussing a topic that is in high demand.

Finding the right price point can be as simple as saying that you want to make three times the cost of your book or maybe you just say that $14.95 sounds good. Or you might take some time and research the market a little deeper. Will you stress out about the price point? Probably. But so does every businessperson on the face of the planet. One general rule of thumb is to set your price on the high-end because you can always offer price reductions if the book isn't selling well.

Michelle Huggins, our author in Chapter One who talked about taking control when you self-publish, was dead-set on selling her hardbound poetry books for $19.95. But when her books came back from the hardback bindery, they looked so good I recommended that Michelle price her book at $24.95. I had no market data to support this recommendation; it was just a gut feeling.

Michelle disagreed with me and so I backed down and wished her luck at her book signing that following Sunday. On Monday morning, I called Michelle and asked her how the signing went. She was ecstatic. She said she sold all 100 hardbound books. I remember cringing inside thinking she should have raised her price. Then she told me that at the last moment she had raised her price to $24.95. By making that last minute decision, Michelle earned an additional $500.

The big wigs who run Corporate America will tell you there is a science to making good decisions. But sometimes you just need to listen to your gut. Michelle listened to her gut and it paid off for her. As a small business owner or book publisher, sometimes all you've got is your gut. Don't be afraid to use it.

As I was researching this topic of deciding the best price for a book, I came across an article that discussed some book pricing statistics published by R.R. Bowker. Bowker is the ISBN agent in the United States and is a reputable organization. I recommend all self-publishing authors to go to www.isbn.org (the Bowker site) as you will find invaluable information.

However, as the following article points out, the statistics R.R. Bowker lists for average book prices may not be the most accurate reference to use when setting the price for your book. One of the main problems when using historical statistics to determine the price of your book is that they may not reflect current market trends. Also, as your search on Amazon and in bookstores will show you, the market price of books is usually a function of a "Retail" price and the subsequent "Discount" price. I highly recommend using the current market price when pricing your book.

Here's the article, paraphrased, from the Book People Archive Bulletin Board. You can read the entire article online at http://onlinebooks.library.upenn.edu/webbin/bparchive

Michael Hart wrote:

We have been VERY conservative as per the "price of the average hardback book," stating it was $40+, when it appears it may be pushing $80 by July 4th, 2006, already well past $70, and that is from last year;

Warning: Bowker's reported the average hardback price at $72.67 for 1997 and $70.05 for 2001, and this figure was reportedly continually decreasing, so this trend may not hit $80, as previous predictions had indicated; a recent phone call indicated this price is now below $70.

Is the average hardback really $40 now? If you ask Bowker's it's much more! About $70...

Total Books

1997	2001 final	2002 final	2003 prelim
$72.67	$70.05	$62.84	$62.94

In 2004, the average suggested retail price for adult hardcovers released by the largest trade houses decreased 10 cents to $27.52; adult fiction hardcovers held steady at $25.08; and adult non-fiction hardcovers decreased 29 cents to $28.49.

Adult trade paperbacks increased 11 cents to $15.76; adult fiction trade paperbacks increased 7 cents to $14.78; adult non-fiction trade paperbacks increased 15 cents to $16.16; and adult mass-market paperbacks increased 14 cents to $7.35. The average list price for juvenile hardcovers increased 26 cents to $16.09.

While this type of information is useful, if you click to the entire article, you will see the historical statistics do not always match up with market reality. When in doubt, go with the market and with your own gut. Remember, you are an independent person and you are in control of your book. No one knows better than you what price you should charge.

Concept Recap

Mindset

The Author's Mindset: I Am Focused, I Am Independent, I Am Innovative, I Am Determined

- Authors need to be like Koko, my Labrador retriever, who has the ability to completely focus on going after something.

- Authors need to fully understand that they are the best salesperson for their book and that ALL authors need to promote themselves, published authors and self-published authors.

- Authors need to learn as FAST as possible how to use the tools available to them today to reach their target audience.

- Authors need to move with a FURIOUS pace to use the tools once they know how to use them.

- As authors, we cannot be like the man digging for treasure who gives up a foot before he reaches his goal.

Publishing

- We discussed the three main ways you can publish your book, Mainstream, Vanity and Self-publishing.

- Each method has pros and cons and the important point is to make an educated decision with your eyes wide open.

- Be wary of the Vanity press and paying a company a lot of money for publishing services, especially if the company will own the rights to your book.

- The type of book you have will help you determine the best type of publishing to pursue.

- The final point is that regardless of which type of publishing you choose, you will need to promote yourself.

Goal Setting and Marketing

- We discussed what a goal is and how to determine the goal or goals for your book.

- We talked about the value of finding your target audience and that the Internet helps you define your target audience quickly.

- We discussed pricing your book and some ways to research books similar to yours to help you choose the right price.

3
Invent Your Strategy
• • •

*Be like a duck, my mother used to tell me. Remain calm on
the surface and paddle like hell underneath.*
– MICHAEL CAINE

I believe we are on the edge of a huge paradigm shift. In the
old paradigm, a few people (publishers) told the market what it
should buy. In the new paradigm, the market will tell us what it
wants and the authors who can effectively provide what the market wants will succeed. The internet gives you direct access to
your market and the authors who learn how to mine this market
will be the ones who will gain the most, either in economic terms
or in humanistic terms; both of which can be equally rewarding.

While all promotional tactics (both online AND offline) should
be used to sell your books, the *DRILL* system is focused primarily on using Internet tools. The Internet is the new frontier for
book promotion and the *DRILL* system helps authors create an
integrated approach to promoting themselves online. One of the
most exciting benefits of online promotion is that the internet
moves at lightening speed so authors can begin *"paddling like hell"*
to start finding readers in their niche market. Another exciting
aspect of the Internet is that you, the author, are in control of
your book's promotional strategy.

The following is a story from a real author who posted his story on www.ezinearticles.com and I liked it so much I posted the article on my own blog, www.howtopublishabookblog.com:

Getting Your Book Published is Only Half the Battle
By Jeffrey Hauser

I once thought I wrote the great American novel. It had all the elements of a success. There was the sympathetic hero that had to face adversity and overcome the bad guys. It was set in rural America and then leapt from coast to coast. It had intrigue, a bit of sci-fi and adventure. It also had a terrific title, "Pursuit of the Phoenix." All my friends and family loved it, so I went searching for a publisher. After failing to find a "normal" publisher like Doubleday and wasting a few bucks on an agent, I went with PublishAmerica for free. Well, not entirely free. I purchased a few hundred copies for my family and myself, but I had a printed book. I was excited to see my name in print.

Let me describe what just happened. I actually self-published using a POD publisher. These kind of businesses print books as they are needed, or "print-on-demand." They store the information like the cover and text on a computer hard drive and then use a mechanical process to make the books one at a time. This method of print is in contrast to a major publisher that will print 1000's for distribution to bookstores throughout the country. The disadvantage with PA and other Pod's is that most bookstores deal directly with wholesalers like Ingrams to get their books. The book chains like Barnes and Noble view POD's like the plague. That's unfortunate and not totally fair. But I'll get back to that. The purpose of this article is to look at marketing. Once you have a book, how do you let people know all about it?

Unless you have someone like Random House pushing it in advertising, you're on your own. I learned the hard way. My book came out in the early 1990's before the Internet took off, so I couldn't spread the word all that easily. Placing ads in the local newspaper can be very expensive. I went to a few bookstores but they weren't interested. Today things are a bit different. For my second book, I went with Booksurge, the publishing division of Amazon.com, the largest bookseller on the net. They placed the book on their site and allowed a link from my site to theirs. They also connect to Barnes and Noble online. This time it was non-fiction; an account of my years as a sales consultant for the Yellow Pages. I did not have to buy any books and they supplied a nice production package for a few hundred dollars. However, I still had to do my own marketing.

But now I had a few options, as do you. I contacted other Yellow Page sites on the web seeing if they would link to my book on Amazon and some did. I then began to write articles about tips regarding the Yellow Pages with links to the book. I go on forums and blogs doing the same thing. Using that method, I've had more sales in a few months than 10 years with my other fiction book. Now I understand that a novel is much harder to sell and accept that eventuality. But the Internet opens up a plethora of opportunities unknown a few years ago. Because I'm letting Amazon sell the copies directly to the public, I don't care that they too are a POD. That's right, Booksurge is a print-on-demand publisher that only prints them as requested. There are no miles of bookshelves in the Amazon warehouse.

But do I really care? I bypass the bookstore that adds a hefty markup and so I am able to price the book lower and still make a few bucks per order. They do all the work as far as taking the credit card, shipping and the paperwork. I just get a royalty check every month. And another thought here. One big advantage to the POD process is that I can update my book's text for a small fee and keep it current because it doesn't sit on the shelf. The printing quality is always excellent and I can also change the cover as well, if desired. My final advice is to issue a press release to all the media when it's published. I got calls from as far away as Australia and London when I sent out my PR's. Good luck and good selling.

Jeffrey Hauser was a sales consultant for the Bell System Yellow Pages for nearly 25 years. He graduated from Pratt Institute with a BFA in Advertising and has a Master's Degree in teaching. He had his own advertising agency in Scottsdale, Arizona and ran a consulting and design firm, ABC Advertising. He has authored 6 books and a novel, "Pursuit of the Phoenix." His latest book is, "Inside the Yellow Pages" which can be seen at his website, http:// www.poweradbook.com/ Currently, he is the Marketing Director for http://www.thenurseschoice.com/ a Health Information and Doctor Referral site.

The "I" in the DRILL System stands for "Invent Your Strategy." You might want to ask me why I've called this *"Invent Your Strategy"* and that would be a good question. My answer is that I do not believe that any ONE strategy will work for all books and I also believe that the only person who can create the right strategy for your book is *YOU.*

The strategy we are talking about in the *DRILL* system is a promotional strategy. We see the Internet as a vehicle for anyone to promote himself or herself. You will not see brash statements by Authors On The Net claiming we can help you sell thousands of books. No one can guarantee book sales. That's why bookstores get to return their unsold books to all the mainstream publishers, you know, those guys who are so good at choosing books that will sell well.

Our intent is to educate authors on the tools they can use to get the word out about their book, because the first reason a book won't sell is that no one knows it exists. Our promise to our customers at Authors On The Net is that if an author uses the tools outlined in this book and on our website, the author will expose his or her book to the marketplace, which is the first step in the book-selling process.

But let's step back a moment and define what strategy means. The dictionary gives the following definition:

> **Strategy:** *a plan, method, or series of maneuvers or stratagems for obtaining a specific goal or result: a strategy for getting ahead in the world.*

"D" in the DRILL system is *Develop Your Goal.* "R" is *Research Your Market.* These two steps need to take place before you can *Invent your Strategy.* Your strategy is your plan of attack and your plan of attack depends wholly on the goal you have set for your book and the audience your book was written for.

Another way of understanding strategy is that strategy bridges the gap between your goals and your tactics. Here are some examples:

- Strategy refers to basic directional decisions, that is, to purposes and missions.

- Strategy consists of the important actions necessary to realize these directions.

- Strategy answers the question: What are the ends we seek and how should we achieve them?

As it is impossible to layout every possible strategy you might implement, the *DRILL* system introduces a "vanilla" strategy any author can use as a foundation for inventing his or her own strategy. How well the strategy works depends largely on how well the plan is executed.

Here's a "vanilla" strategy for our fictitious author Sally:

Goal
Sell 5,000 books

Target Audience:
2.4 million female elementary teachers in the US (3.1 total teachers x 79%, the percent of teachers who are women.

Strategy
Launch a three-phase rollout plan as outlined below:

Phase One
1. Focus on Sally's local market first
2. Sally's local market has 15,000 female teachers
3. Sell 500 books

Phase Two
1. Launch in the three largest markets in the US (San Francisco, Chicago, New York)
2. These markets have a combined female teacher population of 100,000
3. Sell 1,500 books

Phase Three
1. Launch nationwide
2. Sell 3,000 books
3. Sell rights of book to a mainstream publisher

Let's review how Sally's strategic plan fits the definition of strategy. The definition says that a strategy is a plan, method or series of maneuvers to achieve a specific goal. Sally's "series of maneuvers" is to first get her feet wet in her local market. She will learn how to talk to teachers, she will create and hone her tactics and she will begin creating buzz about her book.

Next, Sally will hit the three largest markets. Like any general waging a war, Sally has limited resources, namely time and money. By focusing on the largest markets, Sally will get the biggest bang for her buck. If Sally has $1,000 to spend and she spends it in Ashland, Oregon with 500 female teachers, she will not get as much benefit as if she were to spend that $1,000 in San Francisco with over 5,000 female teachers. In addition, if she can get some traction in San Francisco, the word of mouth buzz might be so great that teachers in Ashland (10 hours by the car to the North) may hear about her book and place orders.

Sally's Phase Three plan is to launch nationwide. If Sally has achieved both her Phase One and Phase Two goals then her book is beginning to show a profit. With these profits, Sally can invest in a large-scale plan to sell her books nation-wide. Even more important than the cash flow is that Sally now knows how to sell her book and she knows that people want to buy her book. Her confidence is strong and she is willing to invest both her time and her money into selling her book on a larger scale.

Sally's strategy fits the definition of what a true strategy should be and with this strategy in place, Sally can make good decisions and spend her resources wisely. In addition, Sally's strategy works as a bridge between her goals and the tactics she will use to achieve her goals.

Many authors and business people (myself included) love tactics. Tactics are action items we write on a piece of paper and check them off when we've completed them. Place book on Amazon—check. Create Book Trailer—check. Strategy helps us make decisions about what tactics are best to help us achieve our goals using our limited resources. Tactics are the hundreds of tools in our toolbox and our strategy helps us choose the tools we need to get the job done right.

Your strategy may be similar to Sally's strategy or it may be entirely different and the tactics you decide to use will vary. For example, if you have a personal adventure story, say a story about how you sailed around the world, your strategy may be to find a distributor who specializes in selling to boat-related outlets around the world. Or your strategy may follow the 3-phase strategy outlined above, focusing first on the US West Coast, then the East coast and then on the Gulf coast.

When you invent your own strategy, you invent your own passion. Your strategy is yours and you own it. You don't wake up in the morning complaining that your plan isn't working, but rather you objectively look at what's not going right and set out to fix it. You take ownership in your plan and you become a truly empowered author.

As a case in point, ask yourself why so many people spend thousands of dollars attending seminars on how to do something like set up an online store or to get rich selling real estate and then end up never implementing one action item they learned in their seminar. You would think that after spending so much money to attend the seminar, people would be invested and do something with what they learned. But 90% of the people do nothing.

I think the reason these people do not take action is that they haven't internalized what they learned. In other words, they haven't made the information they received their own experience. Without making something your own, you won't believe in it and if you don't believe in something, you won't take action on it.

Some authors we work with have thought out their strategy fairly well, but rarely have these authors put an actual plan together with projected sales goals and a roll out plan. Unfortunately, many authors haven't thought much about how to sell their books. In fact, I've personally worked with over 100 authors and not one of these authors has been able to show me their written plan for selling books.

At the time of this edition, a book called *The Secret* is permeating our society. I first heard about this book from the lady who cuts my hair. She loaned me her DVD version of the book. About three days after she loaned me her DVD, my book club sent me a hardcopy version of *The Secret*. The "secret" is about the natural law of attraction and basically says that what we think about, what thoughts we project out into the universe, will attract the resources we need to make our dreams a reality.

With a written goal, a strategy to support that goal and tactics to use to execute the strategy, surprising results can happen. The law of attraction, whether you believe it or not, will kick in and support you in your efforts. By the way, I do believe in the law of attraction, but my belief is that if you are 100% focused on achieving a goal and you are committed enough to *DRILL* that final foot, forces will come to your aid. I am not a big believer in luck, but I am a big believer that hard work done intelligently will generate a "force" and if someone wants to label that force as luck or *The Secret*, that's fine with me.

Going back to Sally's "vanilla" strategy, as Sally starts "paddling like hell" to accomplish her goals, she may get hit with an opportunity completely out of left field. Maybe the Secretary of Education will somehow get a copy of Sally's book and make it mandatory reading for every teacher in the US. Maybe Sally will find that Dallas is a better city to enter than Chicago so she'll change her plan. The point is that Sally has a strategy for her book that will help guide her decision-making and her use of resources and gives her book the best chance for success.

While Sally's "vanilla" strategy illustrates what a strategy should look like, this is Sally's strategy and may not be appropriate for *YOUR* strategy. Each book requires its own strategy, but there is another reason that inventing your own strategy is a more powerful approach than plugging into someone else's "proven" strategy. When you build your own strategy you begin to believe in your strategy and believing in your strategy is the first step to generating attraction.

The author's mindset says that you are independent and innovative. My guess is that if I were to tell authors that I have a system for selling books and if you want to follow my system you have to follow it verbatim (and pay me thousands of dollars), I might get many authors to follow my system but I doubt 100% of these authors would find the success they are looking for. That's why the *DRILL* system is not a rigid system, but rather it is a guideline to help authors create their own strategy.

The Internet tools you will be introduced to in this book and actually shown how to use on our website, www.authorsonthenet.com are just that—tools. The *DRILL* system can introduce you to blogging, how to make a blog and how to get people to your blog, but only you will discover how to take that tool and make something magnificent. For example, I know how to use a hammer, but all I ever do with a hammer is fix things around the house, which is a rare event. Other people with more creativity and a better skill set used a hammer to build the house I live in. Your success using the tools in the *DRILL* system depends on your creativity and in your skill in how you apply the tools.

4

Lay Out Your Tactical Plan

• • •

Strategy without tactics is the slowest route to victory.
Tactics without strategy is the noise before defeat.
– SUN TZU

You have your goal, you know your market and you have your strategy figured out. The next step is to choose the tactics you will use to carry out your strategy and achieve your goals. The next few chapters will lay out a number of tactics you can use including blog sites, websites, social media, online press releases, virtual book tours, book trailers, online bookstores like Amazon and Barnes and Noble, podcasts and others. The bulk of the tactics discussed in *DRILL* deal with the concept of social networking. Effective social networking is the key to building a grassroots movement for your book.

When I first contemplated writing this book, I thought I should title the book something like *1001 ways to sell your book online*. Titles with numbers in them sell really well and my first idea for the book was to list up a bunch of tactics, because as I've said earlier, I love tactics because tactics are action items that bring results.

But as Sun Tzu said, *tactics without strategy is the noise before defeat*. Rattling off a hundred action items will create a lot of "noise," but will those actions generate the results you want? This is one reason I didn't want to simply list up 1001 tactics. Another reason is that to effectively implement many of the tactics in this book will require your focus, your innovativeness and your determination as an independent author.

When we were first launching Razorpages, a partner company to Authors On The Net, I noticed that one of our authors wasn't taking advantage of his blog. At lunch, I explained to him what a blog is and how it can be beneficial to him. He left lunch all excited to start blogging. And he did. He posted an entry and received a few comments, which led to him making a few more posts. Then nothing. I waited a few weeks and still there were no more posts by the author. So I called him up and asked him why he had stopped posting. He said that he hadn't sold any books so he just stopped.

On the other hand, I know an author who has been blogging for over two years, is receiving 3,000 unique visitors a month and is selling books from his blog site. Both authors used the same tactic, but the second author used the tactic much more effectively. This author has spent hours on end on his blog and there were times when he wondered if anyone was ever going to buy his books, but over time, his blog began to deliver results. He kept digging until he found his treasure.

A third reason I chose not to create a laundry list of tactics is that in the online world, tactics come and go at a fast and furious pace. For example, by the time I finished the first draft of *DRILL*, two new tactics for authors were gaining popularity: a social network called Second Life and websites where readers share with others the books they like, which creates an informal book review system.

Because online tactics change so quickly, part of the strategy I've "invented" for *DRILL* is to launch an author community, www.authorsonthenet.com, which will be more effective in helping authors use tactics. Authors can join the website and get up-to-date information on tactics available to promote and sell books. With the book, authors can see how a strategic plan is put together and learn some of the key online tactics to carry out their plan. With the website, authors can stay informed with any new tactics that pop up that might be of use to them.

One of the first online tactics every author should consider is placing his or her book with online bookstores like Amazon.com. While Amazon is the most popular online bookstore, authors have many other places to list their books and one tactic is to put your book on any site that will accept you. Listing your book usually costs little or nothing and is relatively simple to do.

A word of caution: there are pros and cons to each of the services listed below. The good news is that the Internet gives you a quick way to research the company or companies you want to use. For example, one great site is http://www.speculations.com, a place where you can read comments from real people on their publishing experiences.

Another word of caution: do not expect any of the companies listed below to make you successful. Only you can do that. However, if you know exactly what these companies—Amazon, LuLu and Author House, etc.—can and cannot do for you, you employ their services as part of your overall tactical plan and you go about promoting your book on your own, you will have a much richer experience and not go to sleep each night thinking you got ripped off.

The Big Three: Amazon, Barnes & Noble and Borders

While most people today are familiar with Amazon, few authors we work with at ZDocs know about Amazon's Advantage program or how easy it is to set up an account with Amazon. Before we get into how to find the Amazon Advantage program, a point I want to make crystal clear about Amazon and other online retail outlets is that while Amazon is a great site to place your book, Amazon will take 55% of the proceeds when a book sells. In addition, you will need to ship books to Amazon which reduces your net profit further. However, you need to list your book on Amazon as a convenience for your customers and if Amazon finds you a customer, then Amazon deserves its 55%. The caution I make to our authors at ZDocs is to not direct customers you find to buy your book on Amazon. Instead, you want customers to buy your book off of your own blog or website.

To get started using Amazon, go to www.amazon.com and on the home page, click on the "Sell Your Stuff" link. This will take you to the "Make Money" tab and under this tab you will find the "Advantage" program. This is the program you want to sign up for.

If you want to use Borders instead, go to www.borders.com and you will find yourself on the same Amazon site, but instead of being blue, the color scheme is red. When you click on "sell your stuff," you actually go directly to Amazon's site. Instead of reinventing the wheel, Borders teamed up with Amazon.

Barnes and Noble has its own approach to accepting titles and their program is a little harder to find. Go to www.bn.com and find the very tiny "help" word in the upper right-hand corner. Scroll down until you find the section titled "Publishers and Authors" and follow the steps to submitting your book.

Websites are changing all the time, so the actual website navigation may change, but the place you want to find on Amazon is the Advantage program for books and on Barnes and Noble you want the section on becoming a "Vendor of Record." I won't bore you with the details of signing up on these sites as the process is fairly simple and straightforward, but I will encourage you to carefully read all the information about the program before you sign up, especially the terms and conditions of both sites.

Remember what I said in Chapter One about doing those things you least want to do and how that experience will separate you from the herd? Well, reading the user agreements of all the websites you plan to join is a must. Not only will reading these agreements help you avoid costly mistakes, you will learn a great deal about how the websites work and how you can use those tools most effectively.

The reason Amazon is so powerful is that as you read through the documentation, you will find tools that will help you promote your book. The next few paragraphs will briefly explain the different tools available to authors on Amazon.

Amazon Best-seller campaigns

We'll talk later about using email as a way to promote books, but since many people are using Amazon-specific email campaigns, we need to discuss these programs in this section. A year ago I was asked to introduce some of our authors to a person who said they could get an author's book to the number one spot on Amazon. While I was interested in the program, I declined the offer because I didn't want to be responsible for a negative outcome. Usually I'm not so risk-averse, but when it comes to using people's private email lists, caution is required.

Here's how the program works, at least as best as I understand as I've never participated. A "main" author gets other authors—we'll call them sub-authors—to join him or her in an email blast. The sub-authors join the "promoting" author in sending out emails to his or her database. The trick is that each participating author is required to provide enticing give-a-ways to encourage people to go to Amazon and buy the main author's book. *(This is the point where I lost interest, as it seemed to me the only person who was going to become a top seller was the main author. The theory is that every author who participates will benefit, however, an author I know who participated in this program told me she only sold a hundred books while the main author's book became an Amazon best seller. The reason a sub-author might want to participate is they are able to increase their email database when people request the free gift the author is offering.)*

While many book promoting coaches advocate this type of program, many other people are blogging about whether the practice is ethical or not. For example, an author might hit the Amazon best-seller list for an hour in his/her genre. The author will then put on PR pieces that their book is an Amazon best-seller. In my opinion, this is misleading as the author may have only sold a hundred books, but for that one hour on that one day, those 100 book sales put the author's book on the top of the list.

I doubted whether I should even discuss Amazon Best-seller campaigns in *DRILL* as I personally do not advocate using this tactic. I decided to include the tactic for three reasons. First, as authors "invent" their own strategies, some authors may find this program appealing. Second, I would rather an author choose to participate in an Amazon Best-seller campaign with his or her "eyes wide open" rather than to get "sold" into participating. And third, by knowing about the dark side of these campaigns, an author may find a way to use Amazon Best-seller campaigns that are both effective and ethical.

If, after all my words of caution, you are still interested in these types of campaigns and would like to learn more, the following is taken from John Kremer's blog (www.openhorizons.blogspot.com) that sheds more light on these Amazon email campaigns.

> **Question:** Can you please summarize what big mistakes almost all publishers make selling books via an Amazon.com bestseller campaign?
>
> **John's Answer:** The biggest mistake authors or publishers make in trying to become an Amazon.com bestseller is simple: They don't line up enough owners of lists who are committed to sending out the promotional message about the book.
>
> The second biggest mistake: They don't line up enough partners who are giving away something nice for those people who place an order for the author's book.
>
> An Amazon bestseller campaign only works if there are enough bonuses to encourage potential buyers to act right away. And if enough people get the message, the author can make a dent in the Amazon sales.
>
> There is no shortcut to make this happen. You can't rent lists. You can't settle for mailing to just three or four lists. You need at least 15 to 20 lists to make a dent. And you can't provide all the bonuses yourself. That simply does not work because then you do not have any incentive for other list owners to mail to their customers. The only reason a list owner announces a new Amazon.com bestseller book promotion is in the expec-

tation of adding to his or her list via the giveaways that he will send out as part of the overall promotion.

Each participating list owner offers something free— a report, an audio MP3, an e-book—that can be fulfilled via email. When the recipients of the Amazon.com promotion buy the promoted book, they also are sent the other free items, either via a download link at the list owner's site or via email from the list owner providing the free item.

It is the obligation of the person carrying out the promotion to share the emails of everyone who bought a copy of the book as a result of the promotion. It is those email addresses that the various participating list owners can add to their lists.

The list owner, thus, gains two valuable assets by participating in the Amazon.com promotion. 1. He gets to add the names of the people who bought the book (these are good names because they are the names of people who bought via email notice). 2. He gets to expose these buyers to his work via the item that he is giving away free. If your report or e-book is good, chances are that the person will want to buy something else from you.

That's the key elements of a good Amazon.com bestseller promotion. And in almost every case where such a promotion has failed, it's either because there are not enough list owners involved (with a cumulative list total of 100,000 or more) or because the freebies are not enticing enough to get the potential buyer to act right away. In both cases, the fault is in the bookselling promoter who was not willing to go out and sell his promotion to targeted list owners with something valuable to give away to potential buyers (something that the buyers want as much as the promoter's book).

John Kremer http://openhorizons.blogspot.com/ 2005/07/amazon-book-campaigns-why-they-work.html

Again, these types of programs appeal to some people and not to others. For my book, I will not use an Amazon email campaign but rather focus my time and money on other tactics I feel more comfortable with, even if that means my sales may be sluggish or not take off at all. But you may be different. You may love these types of aggressive tactics and that is why this tactic appears as one possible tactic in the *DRILL* system. My only word of caution is to understand the downside as well as the potential upside of this type of marketing.

Amazon's Search Inside Program

When customers search for books on Amazon.com, Amazon uses the actual words from inside your book. For example, if an Amazon customer uses the term "Ambient Marketing" to search for books, Diana Derval's *Wait Marketing* book might pop up as she uses this term frequently in her book. This tool helps customers discover books that may never have surfaced if Amazon just used the author's name, the book title and specific key words. Customers can read your table of contents and a specific item they are looking for might jump out at them causing them to buy your book. You are only showing a few pages, and this can be a great way to get more sales.

Content Acquisition Program (CAP)

I received an email from a customer who was looking for introductions to literary agents. I know only a few literary agents personally and the ones I know are no longer accepting new authors. I referred the customer to the *Writer's Market* book and to a website http://www.e-literaryagent.net/. While these two resources may be helpful, usually the best way to get in with a literary agent is by personal recommendation called Word of Mouth.

The Amazon CAP program was designed to help literary agents and editors find books they may want to publish. Here is the description of how this program works taken directly from Amazon's website:

CAP connects media companies searching for new talent with the thousands of Advantage vendors selling their products on Amazon. As an Advantage vendor and a holder of rights for books, music, or movies, you can select which titles you want in the CAP program and we will include those titles in interactive reports viewed by acquisition editors of media companies, including industry-leading publishers, labels, and studios.

Amazon has long been an advocate of small presses, independent musicians, filmmakers, and self-published authors. As you know, the Advantage program was designed to help these vendors overcome the sales hurdles associated with traditional retail channels and get their products in front of customers worldwide. CAP is designed to help these same vendors market their titles to larger media companies for acquisition. If you are interested in getting your title(s) noticed by a media company, this program is for you.

Getting reviews on Amazon

The easiest way to get reviews on Amazon or anywhere else is to ask for them. While you may receive some spontaneous reviews by customers who buy your book on Amazon, a more aggressive way is to invite everyone who buys a copy of your book to go to Amazon and post a review. A good follow-up tactic is to send each reviewer a thank you card.

We'll be discussing book reviews in more detail in Chapter Seven. In addition, as part of the Authors On The Net community, you can ask other authors for reviews. In fact, we envision a community where an author can conduct quick polls on possible titles for books, book coves and other aspects of publishing where the opinion of others can be beneficial.

Giving reviews on Amazon

Another way to get more traffic to your books is to give reviews on Amazon for similar books or for your competition.

People who look at those books will see your review and may click through to your book or website. Asking for reviews and giving reviews is called social networking, a topic we'll discuss in more detail later.

Your Profile

Another form of social networking on Amazon is creating your profile. Among other benefits, your profile lets you use a tool called *Listmania*. *Listmania* is a great way to showcase a list of books you like and why. You can network with other authors and create lists that include each other's books to help promote each other. You can have as many lists as you like under as many topics as you like. Creating a robust profile can help you network with many other people.

Amazon Marketplace—Sell Your Stuff

You can sell just about anything you want using this function, but since *DRILL* is about promoting books, we'll stick to selling books. You can sell a brand new book, an out of print edition, an autographed copy or a returned or damaged copy and still make some money. If you receive any returns back or have any book copies that are not "perfect" list them on Amazon marketplace for a cheaper price.

Buy X Get Y Program

This program is not for all authors, but if you qualify and have the resources to participate, you may want to look into this program. Again, from Amazon's website:

Welcome to merchandising at Amazon.com!

With dozens of browse categories, thousands of specialized bestseller lists, and advanced search capabilities, Amazon.com gives customers a myriad of ways to find and discover products they'll want to buy. With so many customers and so many products, how do you find your target market? The Buy X, Get Y Program (Paid Placement) is the perfect solution.

The BXGY program allows you to feature your title in the "Best Value" section (also known as "Better To-gether") of another title's detail page. What does this mean? Imagine that you have a book with a similar theme or subject matter to a bestseller such as *Life of Pi*. Now imagine that your title is advertised on this bestseller's page on Amazon.com with a direct link to your title and an additional 5% discount.

If you've ever shopped on Amazon, you've probably seen other titles listed underneath the book you were searching for. These books show up because authors are paying for the placement. One criterion to qualify for the BXGY program is that you must sell less than a million dollars worth of product a year. I think most authors will qualify for this program, but as it is a paid placement program you will need to find out what the costs are and determine if this program is right for you. I recommend you focus on all the free ways to promote your book on Amazon first and once you are comfortable with this tool then take a look at the BXGY program.

Reaching Customers: Personalization & Automerchandising

If you have used Amazon as a customer, you are already familiar with this program. Every time I log into Amazon, Amazon throws up several titles it thinks I will be interested in based on my previous searches and purchases. While we may all be familiar with this tool, this tool is actually what makes Amazon such a powerful sales engine. This tool is similar to the BXGY program, but it is a built-in feature and not a paid program.

• • •

As *DRILL* is not a book on how to be an Amazon Power Seller, I'll stop here. With all the tools Amazon has to offer it is easy to feel overwhelmed. You will need to spend some time getting set up on Amazon and learning how to use the tools to your advantage. Set aside a week and focus on Amazon. Take your time. Read the agreements and all the helpful articles on how to use Amazon.

Amazon is discussed as the first tactic because it is one of the most powerful tools you have in your toolbox. While you will want to sell books directly from your own blog, selling on Amazon is a key success factor for every author. And while Amazon takes 55%, keep in mind that all bookstores take a large percentage of your book's sales and so do distributors. If Amazon can help you sell books, they deserve every penny they earn.

Next we'll discuss a few POD companies you may want to work with. Keep in mind that Amazon also has a POD company called Book Surge. You can find Book Surge by clicking on the "on-demand printing" link from Amazon's main menu.

There are many POD companies you can use and many of these companies have their own bookstores and they will put your book in the Ingram's distribution channel. In addition, most PODs will list your book on Amazon.

One possible strategy is to use a company like LuLu or Author House to publish your book so your book will appear in their online bookstore and on Amazon. If you self-publish and have your own ISBN, you can list your book on Amazon but not with many of the other POD companies as they will only list books with their own ISBNs.

The purpose of introducing the next few companies is to give you an idea of the POD companies you can choose from and to help you make good decisions should you choose to go this route. The best book I can recommend to help authors choose among the many PODs is by Mark Levine and is titled *"The Fine Print of Self-Publishing."* (http://www.book-publishers-compared.com/)

LuLu.com

I've spent a lot of time on LuLu's site and my opinion is that LuLu is a great enabler for the self-publishing author. What this means is that when you use LuLu you are in total control of the process. You decide what kind of product you want to sell, you upload your files and you choose your price. In addition, I haven't found any negative feedback from the Internet regarding LuLu's services.

To explain all the cool things you can do on LuLu, I'd have to write another book. So I'll just summarize my evaluation of LuLu and encourage you to go to www.lulu.com and review their offering for yourself. First of all, LuLu makes the self-publishing process very easy and many of our authors on Razorpages will direct their readers to LuLu to buy their books. Second, LuLu offers a storefront where readers can find and buy books, which is a nice feature but in no way replaces the need to put your books on Amazon.

The only negative I have experienced with LuLu is that a book I ordered looked very "self-published." The binding was not crisp and the inside pages looked as if the author had spent no money to have the manuscript edited and formatted. LuLu will print whatever you, the author, want them to print. This is LuLu's business model and it works for them and thousands of authors.

When authors print with ZDocs, we try hard to help them make their books look professionally published because that is our business model. We print fewer books than LuLu so we can take a more consultative approach. But if one of our authors says to print, we will go ahead and print what the author wants because just like LuLu, we are in the business of supporting self-publishing authors. Some authors may not have the time or money to make their book look more professional and the added investment may not earn them a higher return. Those decisions are the authors to make, not the printing company's to make.

Author House

Author House is one of the largest self-publishing companies in the US and its product offering is similar to LuLu. However, to get started on LuLu requires no signed agreements or any money down, but with Author House, you are required to purchase at least $600 worth of services.

Another difference is that Author House will work with the author to make his or her book look like a published book. With LuLu, you upload your files for them to print. With Author House, you submit your manuscript and then their design team formats your book. This is why you pay money up front to get started and you pay more to have your cover designed and your book edited.

As with Amazon and LuLu, be sure to read all the agreements with Author House so you know what you are getting into. Author House has all their agreements available online for you to download and read before you decide to use them. While Author House has thousands of satisfied customers, I have heard negative comments about Author House, so if you do decide to go with Author House, just be sure you know exactly what you are getting into. The key is to understand the contracts and have a clear picture of what Author House will and will not do for you. The main advantage I see with Author House is their expertise in helping you print a professional-looking book.

While Author House will sell you on their ability to help you sell books, I would caution you against getting your hopes up because I have yet to find a sure-fire system guaranteed to sell books. You, the independent author, will invent your own strategy for selling books and you won't rely on any third party's claims that they can sell books for you. You may decide to use Author House or LuLu or ZDocs, but you will do so knowing that your book will sell only if you personally promote it.

BooksJustBooks.com

Another company that is reputable and one I recommend you review is www.BooksJustBooks.com. As with Author House and LuLu, I will simply recommend you go to the BooksJustBooks site and spend some quality time learning about their services. As you look at all these sites, you will see how similar their product offerings are and you will also get a feel for how they are different.

Before moving onto the next company, I want to point out that an author does not have to choose just one company to work with. You may need to choose just one company for economic reasons, but if possible, use all these companies or a mixture of them. For example, you can use Author House, LuLu, ZDocs and of course, Amazon if you wish and your book will be on four separate websites. Depending on which companies you work with, you may have some limitations put on your ability to sell in different channels. Read the agreements carefully before signing.

To illustrate this point, ZDocs has an author who first printed with Book Surge (a POD company owned by Amazon), and then printed with LuLu and then printed with ZDocs. When I asked her why she printed with ZDocs, she said price. This author is in Salt Lake City, Utah so being local gave us an advantage over LuLu and Book Surge. In addition, LuLu and Book Surge both print with the same printer, Lightening Source, so these two companies are basically reselling the books. ZDocs, on the other, actually prints its own books so we have a cost advantage. ZDocs can also give this author more personalized attention.

While I'd like to tell everyone to print with ZDocs, the truth is that authors have many choices. Making the right choice can be difficult, but if you were to start your printing project by approaching Book Surge, LuLu, Author House and ZDocs, you will be well on your way to figuring out the best company or companies to print with.

Publish America

Publish America (www.publishamerica.com) sounds like the perfect choice for most authors. They pay you money if they accept your manuscript. But as with most offers that sound too good to be true, the devil is in the details. As I do not have any experience with Publish America, I cannot say whether their service is right for you or not, but I can direct you to some places on the web besides their website that will shed some light on how their service works and whether it is right for you. As you read these reviews, keep in mind that Publish America publishes over 4,800 titles per year. Of these 4,800 authors, you would think there would be some success stories so I encourage you to look for those stories.

The first place I'd go is http://www.speculations.com/
?t=102187. You can also go to "Why We Don't Recommend
PublishAmerica" at AbsoluteWrite and to Writer Beware and
Preditors & Editors and to Publish America Sucks. These sites are,
as you can see, not going to be recommending Publish America.

When I typed in my Google search bar "Success Stories with
Publish America," an article in the Washington Post by Paula Span
was the top result. While I'd like to reprint Paula's article, I did not
receive permission, so what I will do is introduce the article and
how you can go find it yourself. To paraphrase, the story Paula
Span tells is of a lady named St. Amour, who was thrilled to find
out that a "publisher" had accepted her book for publication.

> In June, a publisher in Frederick, Md., agreed. "I'm happy
> to inform you that PublishAmerica has decided to give
> your Bare Bones the chance it deserves," it announced
> via e-mail. "To say I was excited is an understatement.
> I've wanted to be published my entire life," recalls St.
> Amour, who is 31. "I called everyone I could get on the
> phone; I e-mailed everyone I knew."

But as Paula Span reported, the author soon became skeptical
at how Publish America was going to help her sell books. Paula
reported:

> Doubts first arose when she [St. Amour] began receiv-
> ing e-mailed exhortations offering special, limited-time
> discounts if she agreed to purchase many copies of her
> own book. Would Avon or Pocketbooks do that? She
> wondered. She grew suspicious, too, when the proofs
> of her novel arrived—riddled, St. Amour says, with spell-
> ing, punctuation and grammatical errors.

What interested me when I was looking over Publish
America's website was how they said the author pays nothing
and that the author must be responsible for promoting his or her
own book. I had the impression that Publish America was being
upfront and absolutely honest in their approach. But based on
the Washington Post story, the way Publish America makes their

money is to entice authors to buy their own books.

Publish America may be a great choice for many authors, I can't say. I can say that there is a lot of bad press out there on Publish America and many other companies. My intent here is to simply say that whether Publish America or any other company is right for you is up to you. Read the agreements. Do Google searches and find out what others are saying about the company you are thinking of using. Before choosing any company, know up front what you are going to get and what you are going to have to do to make yourself successful.

The Washington Post article I found, by the way, is:

> **Making Books**
> Self-publishing companies are in the business of selling dreams. But what if the dream becomes a nightmare?
> *By Paula Span*
> Sunday, January 23, 2005; Page BW08

Other Places

There are other, less well-known companies out there selling books online. I recommend you go directly to http://archive.museophile.org/bookstores/ to see a complete list of online bookstores. I have clicked through just about every single store on this site and the list below represents those online bookstores that accept book submissions by self-publishers. As a part owner in Razorpages, I highly recommend you list your book at www.razorpages.com as the service is free and the unique aspect of Razorpages is that the site is a book promotion site rather than a book-publishing site or just a bookstore. Here's the short list of places authors should consider placing their books:

- **A1 Books.**

- **www.amazon.com** and any international affiliate like **www.amazon.co.uk**

- **www.barnesandnoble.com** Booksellers, USA. Over 400,000 in-stock books Search over 1 million titles. Includes an on-line live events, book forum, etc. (free registration).

- **Book Passage**, Corte Madera (near San Francisco), California, USA. (This site is a little different, but I thought it might be useful to some authors)

- **Books AtoZ** publishing resources.

- **BookWire**, the book industry resource.

- Razorpages. **www.razorpages.com**

Audio books:

- **Audio Book Club.**

- **AudioBooks Online.**

- **Audio BookWorld.**

- **Audio Publishers Association**

And here are some sites I never would have thought of if I hadn't stumbled upon them at **www.booksellingonlineblog.com:**

- **www.craigslist.org**

- **www.kijiji.com**

- **www.facebook.com**

- **www.internetbooksellers.net**

Remember, websites change all the time. Hopefully when you are reading this book, these sites will still be around but don't be surprised if some sites are no longer active. The point, however, is the web offers authors many places to sell their books. Choose the places you feel most comfortable with.

Summary

When you start looking into all the possible places to "place" your book, keep in mind the differences between mainstream publishing, vanity publishing and self-publishing. Companies like Author House, ZDocs, Amazon and Lulu may be good companies to use, but use them with your *"Eyes Wide Open."* While you will find negative comments from authors who have used these services, keep in mind that these author's negative experiences may be because what they *thought* they were getting into was not what the company was really offering.

The bottom line is that regardless of what services you choose to use, you will need to promote yourself and my research tells me that few companies specialize in helping you promote your books. Once you have listed your book on as many online stores as possible, you can use the *DRILL* system outlined in this book and our website, www.AuthorsOnTheNet.com to promote your book.

Offline Book Sales

DRILL is heavily skewed to online promotional tactics. The main reasons we have chosen to focus our service offering on online promotional techniques is (1) online tools offer authors low-cost tactics to drill into their target audiences, (2) traditional distribution channels are already well entrenched and entering that market would be costly, (3) selling online is an efficient use of time and (4) offline book stores are shutting 50% of their "brick and mortar" locations.

But while the DRILL system is biased toward Internet promotional tools, using traditional methods to get your books in bookstores and on other "real-world" shelves is a big part of drilling until you find your treasure. For example, Michelle Huggins struck gold when she sold all 100 of her hardbound poetry books at a single book signing in a specialty bookstore in Park City, Utah. Her book won't be a best seller, but she cleared over $1,000 in profits. For many self-publishers, that's not bad.

Once you get your creative juices flowing, both online and offline, you will begin to discover many possible places to sell your book. And like our author Irv Cohen who discovered his poetry books sell well in retirement homes, as you set about finding places to sell your book, you may discover some unique sales outlets you hadn't thought about while making your plan.

Another reason we chose to focus on Internet promotional tools is that other people can help authors distribute their books in more traditional ways better than we can. Companies like Ingrams, for example. One book I highly recommend every author read is a book by Brian Jud titled *Beyond the Bookshelf*. In his book, Brian lists 79 strategies for selling books in non-traditional ways. You can buy his book by going to http://www.bookmarketingworks.com

When thinking about the many "places" to sell your books, you do not want to limit your book sales to just online or offline places. Likewise, when planning on how to promote your books, you want to plan on both online and offline tactics. The remainder of this book focuses on what online tactics you can use to promote your book both fast and furiously.

Concept Recap

Strategy

- Strategy is *a plan, method, or series of maneuvers or stratagems for obtaining a specific goal or result: a strategy for getting ahead in the world.*

- Strategy is a bridge between your goals and the tactics you will use to achieve your goals.

- The value of having a book promotion strategy is you will use your limited resources—time and money—more efficiently.

- Inventing your own strategy is not difficult or time consuming and having your own strategy gets the buy-in of the most important stakeholder—you.

Tactics—Part I

- One of the first actions to take is to make your book available in as many online sales channels as possible—starting with Amazon.

- Amazon has the most robust service on the Internet and every author should become expert Amazon sellers.

- Other places to consider are Barnes & Noble, LuLu, Author House and Razorpages.

5

What My Sushi Chef Taught Me About Blogging

• • •

This notion of self-publishing, which is what Blogger and blogging are really about, is the next big wave of human communication. The last big wave was Web activity. Before that one it was e-mail. Instant messaging was an extension of e-mail.
– ERIC SCHMIDT

I lived in Japan over twelve years and during that time I traveled quite a bit throughout Asia. As many people who worked with me will attest, I like to eat and while I may not be the most adventurous eater, I have tried many different cuisines and I have concluded that my favorite food is sushi.

One aspect of Asian dining is the style of eating is very social. In Korea, we often sat around a table cooking our food in front of us while interacting with family, friends or colleagues. In China or Taiwan, the food is brought out and placed in the middle of the table and everyone eats from all the dishes. Again, this style of eating promotes more social interaction than the Western style of one plate per one person does.

One reason I like sushi is the social aspect of most sushi bars. There's a restaurant in the Treasure Island hotel in Las Vegas that is actually called a "Social Sushi" restaurant. I went there with some colleagues and while the atmosphere was nice and the sushi not too bad, I thought the place was too large and not nearly as social as my favorite sushi bar in Tokyo. "My" sushi bar is called Sushi Toshi and whenever I travel to Tokyo, Sushi Toshi is usually my first stop after checking into my hotel.

Sushi Toshi has a horseshoe counter and no dining tables. The horseshoe shape ensures that the Master and his chefs can see the faces of their patrons at all times. Although I haven't been to Japan in a couple of years, I know that if I were to walk into Sushi Toshi today, the Master, Mori sensei, would break into a large smile and say "Irashaimase!"—Welcome!

I have been visiting Sushi Toshi on and off for over 12 years. Mori sensei knows a lot about me and even if we haven't seen each other for a while, it doesn't take us long to catch up. But my social interaction isn't just with Mori sensei. Sitting at the counter, I usually interact with the people sitting next to me and sometimes with people on the opposite side of the counter, depending on how the conversation flows.

A sushi bar as a metaphor for blogging conveys the point that what happens in the offline world is not really that different from what happens in the online world. With a restaurant, there is a theme, which for Sushi Toshi is sushi, of course. People gather at Sushi Toshi to eat sushi, but they also gather to do more than that. They gather to interact. They want to talk about sushi, the intricacies of how to make good sushi and what fish is currently in season. Some customers think they are experts and enjoy the chance to show off their knowledge.

> **Point 1:** Make your blog devoted to one theme, which for an author is the theme of the book. Don't vary from your theme.

When you walk into Sushi Toshi, you realize that people are not there to simply eat. They want to interact with other people. Mori sensei knows this about his clientele and designed his restaurant to cater to the desire his customers have to socialize. The real dynamic that is happening in Sushi Toshi is that people are connecting with other people. It doesn't take long for conversations to spontaneously spring up. And often, when the people sitting next to me at the counter get ready to leave, we'll exchange business cards, a common practice in Japan, and exchanging business cards or phone numbers is a lot like linking on a blog site.

Many of us have a place where we feel comfortable and where we like to interact socially with others. Maybe your favorite place is a bar or coffee shop or your church. Authors and readers should feel as comfortable on a blog site as they do sitting in his or her favorite Sushi restaurant or bar or coffee shop. There isn't much difference really, except when you blog you interact through a computer and when you go into your favorite "joint" you interact face-to-face. The same basic rules apply because what you are doing in both instances is developing relationships.

Point 2: Encourage interaction with visitors to your site.

My blog site (www.howtopublishabookblog.com) has always been a professional site (versus a personal site like many people have on MySpace) and so I have interacted with visitors to my blog as I would interact with anyone professionally. If someone takes the time to link to me, I evaluate their site and if it is appropriate I link to them. If someone were to leave me a negative comment, I would respond honestly and openly and try to resolve the problem. If someone leaves me a question, I do my best to respond quickly.

> **Point 3:** Find your voice. A professional site has one type of voice, a news site has another type of voice and a personal opinion site has a different type of voice. For example, if I were to say, "yo, babe, this site is blankety blank hot. Check it out!" I would not be consistent with my general professional voice, but if I had a personal site where I directed 20 some-things to popular places around town, that voice might be absolutely appropriate.

I do my best to write relevant content because when a search engine plops someone on my site, I'm hoping my content will attract their attention and answer a question they might have. I realize that most people are looking for free information and so I am willing to share whatever knowledge I may have and at the same time I'm not shy about letting my visitors know what I do and that I would love to have them as a customer, but the sale's pitch is very soft, like background music in a restaurant.

> **Point 4:** Selling on a blog is generally a soft sell. People are going to go to their search engine and type in a key word to find information to help them. The expectation on the net is that we can get the information we need for free. You want your visitors to find information that helps them, but you also want them to know that you have other products or services they can use for a fee.

Another important rule of blogging etiquette is that I never use anyone else's information without giving them proper credit. The Internet is full of free information and a lot of it is available for you to use, but to use it ethically, you need to link back to the author. This is one of the rules we'll talk about later when we talk about Search Engine Optimization, or SEO.

While we are on the subject of ethics, one big difference between socializing online versus socializing offline is transparency. Offline, people can see you and if you do something rude like punch the person next to you, the offended person can take swift and immediate action. Online socializing, for some odd reason, tempts people to be fake. You can fake comments. You can spam. You can buy programs to generate thousands of fake links. While some of these tactics may bring you success in the short-run, in the long-run they are recipes for failure. If you will take some time and honestly socialize, you will get the results you want. Think like you are sitting in your favorite "place" and you will know the proper ways to socialize online.

> **Point 5:** Never plagiarize others. Don't spam. Don't buy links. Don't pay for bogus comments. Unethical socializing is the kiss of death.

Three years ago when we decided to start using the Internet as the primary way to promote ZDocs, I had one primary fear.

That fear was that we wouldn't be able to develop strong customer relationships and I felt that the primary distinguishing characteristic ZDocs had was that we built strong bonds with our customers. My fear was totally unnecessary.

Today, we have customers in Canada, Massachusetts, Seattle, Amsterdam and Germany and I feel a close bond with each of these customers. I've even met several of them. One customer from Seattle happened to be in Salt Lake seeing her mother and so Ben (the ZDocs' customer service rep who helped her with her book) and I took her out to—that's right—sushi.

When writing this book, I have assumed that my readers will be at different comfort levels when talking about promoting on the Internet. Some authors reading this book may not have a computer, although this particular group of readers is an ever-diminishing crowd. Many people today have heard about blogging, but few people, relatively speaking, operate a blog. The number of people getting set up on a blog is growing each day, but many of these people do not know the intricacies of how to drive traffic to their blog site, something we call SEO and social networking. Of course, there is also a large number of people who do blog regularly and who do have a good idea how to optimize their site. Regardless of what level you may be at, the one concept I hope you take away from this chapter is that blogging is nothing more than humans connecting with each other.

One of the greatest lessons Mori sensei taught me in his sushi bar is that a well-run business is a business that is personal. Too many companies are so large these days they rely heavily on "systems" to run their businesses and they are forgetting how to be personal.

Have you ever wondered why we hate those automated phone systems? Have you ever found yourself swearing at the computer-generated voice telling you "she" didn't understand what *YOU* said? And you're the human. We dislike these automated phone systems because they are impersonal.

The way ZDocs, a little company in Salt Lake City, Utah, earned the trust of authors all over the states and even outside of the states is by doing one thing very well. That one thing is that we respond to all inquiries within 24 hours and after we respond, we follow-up a few days later. The best way to give your blog site or web site a personal touch is to respond in a timely manner. I think it is safe to say that responding in a timely manner is common-sense etiquette in the offline world, but I'm afraid in the online world quick responses are an anomaly.

Point 6: Selling online is personal

You can gain a great advantage over your competitors by responding in a timely manner. You can also attract customers by having sincere interactions with people online and the best method for creating this personal, online interaction is with a Blog site.

Your Blog Site

All authors need a blog site and their blog site should act as the centerpiece for all their promotional activity. For example, if Sally (remember our fictitious author from Chapter Two?) is planning a road trip to attend regional school district conferences where she can promote her book, she can announce her schedule on her blog and not only will potential customers see that she is coming to a town near them, she can direct people to her blog when she sends out press releases. As you move throughout the rest of this book, I hope to show how a blog site, while it should not be your only marketing activity, should be the centerpiece of your marketing activity.

Starting a blog is not difficult and does not cost a lot of money. In fact, if you use the Google-owned Blogger.com or WordPress, your blog site will not cost anything at all as these services are free. If you choose to use Typepad by SixApart, you'll pay about $159.00 for a year subscription. Authors On The Net introduces authors to WordPress as it is a free service and it gives you all the functionality you will need to effectively blog.

Blog is the shortened word most commonly used for Web Log. A web log—Blog—is a mix between a website and a chat room, but one of the main differences is the ability to syndicate a blog using RSS feeds. If you want to get an in-depth look into blogging,

I recommend you buy and read the book, Blog Marketing by Jeremy Wright (http://www.blogmarketingbook.com/). If you want to see some good blogs right now, I recommend you visit the following sites:

www.where-to-now.com

www.howtopublishabookblog.com

www.kathyholmes.net

www.hidingfromhope.blogspot.com

The main question I want to address is why a blog site needs to be the centerpiece for marketing your book. The reason is SEO. SEO stands for Search Engine Optimization. Almost anyone can start a website, but the trick is getting people you want—your target audience—coming to your website. We'll discuss some general SEO concepts in this chapter and then look at some blog-related SEO skills in Chapter 6.

If you start a traditional website, you have two primary ways to get your target audience to your site. One way is called pay-per-click. Have you ever searched for anything on Google? When you conduct a search, you will usually see three sections on your results page. The first section is the gray area on top, which contains the top two or three results of your search. The second area is the side bar on the right. These two sections contain links to sites and if you click on these links then the company will pay Google for directing traffic to their site.

The third area is what is called the "organic" area. This section is the white space under the gray space and to the left of the side bar. If you click on one of these links, the company you are directed to does not pay Google. The most coveted place on Google or any search engine is the top four places in this organic space.

As you might imagine, capturing one of these four spots in the organic area is not easy. To show up there, companies generally have to pay someone to optimize their website. I've received bids up to $120 per page and since you need at least 100 pages to get the results you want, you're going to need to spend around $12,000 to correctly optimize your website. So even though you may not have to pay Google or Yahoo a fee for each click through, you will still be paying someone to optimize your site to show up in one of those top four places.

Blog sites work a little differently. One of the key ways to optimize any website is to have many pages of content that is relative to a person's search. The same theory holds true for Blog sites. For example, my blog is all about publishing and book promotion. The words publishing and books and authors appear in just about every entry I make. Currently, I have over 250 posts and I add at least one new post each day. One way I am able to post each day is that I place articles by other people (I find these articles on www.ezinearticles.com) as well as posts I write myself. But I only get good optimization for the posts I originate. The search engines know when the same content is duplicated and only the originator gets credit. I don't mind putting other people's articles on my site because I am writing a lot of my own content and I want these other articles on my blog so visitors can get the information they are looking for.

When a person searches for book publishing, there is a good chance my blog site will appear high up on the search engines and the probability I will appear increases with every post I make, especially the posts that originate with me. In other words, I don't have to pay someone to help me optimize my blog because through the natural act of posting content relevant to the theme of my blog, I am doing my own SEO.

Another key SEO element of blogging is the social interaction called linking. On just about any blog site, you will see a list of links the author has put on his or her sidebar. Every time a fellow blogger puts your blog on his or her blogroll (that's what you call the list of links on the sidebar) your SEO is improved. In addition, if anyone happens to mention your blog in one of their own posts, the search engines recognize this as a link as well.

To summarize, two key ways to optimize your blog site is to have a lot of content, which means you need to post a lot, and have lots of links, which means you need to socialize with other bloggers. The key is that by doing these two activities you are in control of your own SEO and that is the secret of blogging and that is why you are better off making your blog the centerpiece of your marketing activities rather than a traditional website.

But there is more. One of the main differences between a website and a blogsite is that you can syndicate a blog by using RSS. RSS stands for Really Simple Syndication. Sydication means that people can subscribe to your blog. When someone subscribes to your blog, every time you create a new entry, your information will download to their feedreader, which is located on their desktop. The reader never needs to come to your blog again because your blog—your entries—will go to the reader.

One aspect of SEO you might want professional advice with is setting up your Meta Tags and Keywords correctly. Meta Tags and Keywords help search engines find your site and there is a science behind how search engines work and the search engine companies like Google change the rules from time to time. I am not an SEO expert so I hire experts to correctly set up my SEO. For $500, you can find professionals to set up your SEO and I highly recommend using experts unless you understand search engine optimization thoroughly.

A lot of authors we work with already have a website and if you happen to have a website that's great because you now have another tool. Besides different ways to optimize, websites and blog sites have one other key difference. That difference is that the content on a blog site is always changing, that is, if you are constantly blogging the most recent article will appear at the top of the screen and older entries will be "pushed" down.

Content on a website is fairly static and only changes when you decide to make a change, which for most people is fairly infrequent. You can place static content on a blog site also, but usually only on the top and side bars and on pages you create. To see the difference between websites and blogsites, simply go to a few websites and a few blog sites and you will see how the latest blog entries on the blog sites are at the top of the screen and the older ones are further down the screen and you'll see the content on the websites as static information that will be there every time you load the website.

If you do not already have a website, I wouldn't bother making one, at least not until you fully developed your blog site and for some reason you want to also have a website. Having both is fine, but both tools have an associated cost with them in terms of either time or money or both, so that is why I recommend the blog site first, and then, if necessary, a website. A substitution for a website, by the way, is a landing page. A landing page is static like a website and it has a very specific purpose, like selling a product. A landing page is like an online brochure and can be a very effective tool.

An example might help to clarify the subtle differences between websites and blog sites and how you might use each tool to your advantage. ZDocs currently has three websites and a blog site. One website is www.zdocscolorprinting.com another is www.zdocsbooks.com and the third is www.zdocsonline.com. The blog site is www.howtopublishabookblog.com.

The www.zdocsonline.com site is our primary "work" site. This is the site where customers request estimates, send files and find out more about ZDocs. The www.zdocscolorprinting.com website is used to promote our color products. We send out direct mail pieces to get people to come to this site to learn in more detail what our capabilities are and to get them to place a bid request. The www.zdocsbooks.com website is focused on selling book printing. I spent less than $2,000 to create each website and I created these websites myself and I have no idea what html or asp or php code is. You don't need to know programming to create your own website these days and the main advantage besides the low cost is that you are in total control of your content.

As the information for selling color printing and books can stay pretty static, we use websites. In addition, a blog site talking about color printing services would be extremely boring. Ditto for a blog site talking about ZDocs. Blogs would not be the best tool to sell color printing or to be the customer interface for receiving jobs and so forth. That's why we use websites.

A key point for a website or a blog to be effective is that its message and purpose need to be focused, especially websites or blogs that are being used for marketing. That's why the focus of the ZDocs Blog is books and the www.zdocscolorprinting.com website is for color products like postcards and brochures.

If you are an author with several books, you will need to invent your blogging strategy. For example, if your books are all non-fiction books on basket-weaving, then one blog discussing the topic of basket-weaving might be your choice. Or if you have one book on basket-weaving and your other book is a spy novel, then operating two blogs might be your choice. There are two main reasons you want to be as focused as possible on the web. The first reason is that people will be conducting searches using specific keywords and the second reason is that people generally stay only seconds or minutes on a website or blog. If that person who just landed on your page does not see what he or she is looking for, they click away immediately.

So far we've been talking about SEO or Search Engine Optimization, which is a way to "organically" get people to come to your website or blog site. Organically means you don't pay a search engine when someone clicks through to your site. Another way to get people to your site is to use pay-per-click. You may have heard of Google ad words and this is a type of pay-per-click advertising and pay-per-click, or PPC, is a powerful tool for many websites.

For example, ZDocs has had great success using pay-per-click campaigns. The reason this marketing tactic works so well for ZDocs is that on any given day there are millions of authors searching the web for places to print their books. If my daily budget is $50.00, I will get about 10 potential customers clicking through to my site each day and of these 10 potential customers about one person will request an estimate and I can usually close several customers a week and the profits from just two of these customers is enough to pay for my entire advertising expense for the month.

So if PPC works so well for ZDocs, why am I not recommending this tactic for authors? The reason is the size of the typical author's target audience and the amount of revenue that can be earned on each closed sale. Compare the following two examples:

The ZDocs PPC tactic:

Monthly budget:	$1,500
Daily pay-per-click usage:	$50.00
Average number of daily click-throughs:	10
Average number of daily bid requests:	1
Average number of closed sales:	.5
(or 1 every other day, 30 days a month or 15 orders each month)	
Average Sales per customer:	$1,000
Total Sales per month:	$15,000

If I gross 50% on each sale, my Internet campaign earns me $7,500. When I subtract the $1,500 I spent on my PPC campaign, I net $6,000. Obviously I can't run a business on $6,000 net income a month, but in reality two things happen that keeps me in business. First, many of these customers become repeat customers so I get a snowball effect. Second, every now and then I hit pay dirt, which means a large corporate publisher finds us and these corporate publishers spend tens of thousands of dollars each year. So a PPC campaign works miracles for a small company like ZDocs.

Now let's look at how a pay-per-click campaign would NOT work for an author:

Monthly budget:	$1,500
Daily pay-per-click usage:	$50.00
Average number of daily click-throughs:	10
Average number of book purchases per day:	1
Average Sales per customer:	$15.00
Total Sales per month:	$450
Net Loss:	$1,050

The actual numbers are not important, but what is important is to understand the concept. The concept is this: it costs anywhere from $1.00 to $5.00 every time someone clicks on your pay-per-click link and only a small percentage of the people who do click on your link will actually pay you money. So for a company like ZDocs that has a fairly high sales ticket ($1,000 on average for each customer) PPC works. But for small ticket items like books, PPC generally does not generate a sufficient return on investment.

> **Point 7:** Blogging is a way for anyone to attract traffic to his or her site and since it costs nothing more than maybe 30 minutes a day of the author's time, if a person comes and doesn't buy, it isn't going to put the author in the red.

The magic of Internet advertising is that you can drill into your target audience. If you have a book on teaching people how to prepare sushi in their own homes, your target audience may only be 10,000 people in the entire world. The Internet gives you the ability to make your book available to all 10,000 people, assuming they have an Internet connection and they are motivated enough to conduct a search for making sushi at home.

The first key is getting people to your site. Chapters 6 and 7 introduce some of the key online tactics you can use to get people to your site. Getting visitors to actually buy something—your book—is a topic we will discuss heavily on Authors On The Net. Here, I will simply explain what converting is and tell one story from my own blogging experience.

Marketing is knowing who your customers are, Promoting is telling the world about your product and Converting is selling. Converting is the ability to turn a visitor to your site into a paying customer. *DRILL* is focused on Promoting, or getting people to your site because authors can't sell books if no one knows their book exists. But what we really want is to sell books.

Selling books is a more complicated topic because often no one—and I include publishers when I say no one—knows if people will buy an author's book. Timing seems to play an important role in actual book sales. Luck may play an even bigger role. While most best-selling books have a good message or story and are well-written, millions of other well-written books with a good message or story do not sell too well. Moby Dick, for example, was a dismal seller when it came out, but years after its first publication and the death of its author, it started selling and eventually became a classic and was even made into a movie. Serendipity is a word authors will become intimate with.

As we build our community on Authors On The Net, one goal is to create a knowledge-base of ideas authors have used to sell books. Some good examples are how Richard Paul Evans ran his book campaign like a political campaign. Another good example is how the creators of *The Secret* developed a grass roots movement; a movement some say was started because they designed packaging to create a connection between *The Secret* and *The Da Vinci Code*.

My conversion story is much more humble. I blogged every day for about three months but no one was requesting an estimate to print books. I had put the exact same "Request Estimate" page on my blog as I had on my website, but no one was using it. On the top of my sidebar on the left, I had a description of what the ZDocs Blog was all about. I thought visitors would want to know what to expect from my blog.

One day I was meeting with the Buzz Booster ladies, Shahar and Nash, and Nash suggested I put a simple form in place of my ZDocs introduction. Nash explained that the most valuable "real-estate" on a blog is the upper left hand area. The day after I put this form up, I received a legitimate request. I now get several requests a week. You can see this form by going to www.howtopublishabookblog.com.

Again, the topic of conversion is too big to discuss in *DRILL*, which is more about how to get visitors to your site in the first place. I encourage you to visit Authors On The Net and join the forum and participate in the "converting visitors to customers" thread. In addition, spend some time on other author blogs and see what they are doing to sell their products. You will see many calls to action like signing up for newsletters and downloading free audio clips or PDF files. The trick is finding what works for you and your book.

6
DRILL Bits

• • •

Opportunities multiply as they are seized.
— SUN TZU

Sun Tzu, that great Chinese strategist, had no idea what Search Engine Optimization (SEO) was when he said, "Opportunities multiply as they are seized." And yet, his words are as true on the blogger's battlefield today as they were on the warrior's battlefield in his time.

This chapter focuses on getting people to your blog. While the final treasure you are digging for is someone willing to give you cash for your book, in order to sell books you first need to get people to know your book exists. One of the great benefits of a blog site is that you can, on a daily basis, see how many people are visiting your site. You can track your visitors and see what keywords they use to find your site. You can find out if your visitors are coming from Canada or Japan or from Mississippi.

In Chapter 5, we introduced several key concepts regarding SEO, which is all about helping search engines direct people to your blog. For your website, using an SEO expert is a good idea if you have the budget. I do not recommend an SEO expert to try to "trick" the search engines, but rather to ensure your site is optimized to make it easy for the search engines to find.

For blogs, I recommend you get started, blog and social network for a few months and if you are not getting the results you want, consult with a SEO expert to see if he or she can help increase traffic to your site. For my blog, 18% of my traffic comes from the search engines and over 60% comes from social networking. In addition, search engines may be bringing the wrong people to my site, but people who visit through social networking are generally people who can benefit most from my blog and people who will hopefully need my services one day.

The following 10 tactics are a mixture of SEO and social networking techniques you can use on your own to bring the right traffic to your blog.

Tactic 1: Write new content frequently

When I launched my first blog, www.sellingbooks.blogs.com, I wrote vigorously for about 30 days and since I didn't know about Ezines and how to load up content from other authors, everything I wrote on my blog was original content. After a few weeks of posting like a mad duck, I went to the Technorati search engine and typed in self-publishing. I was astounded to see that of the 19 entries that popped up on the first page, 12 were from my blog.

When you are first getting started, you should try to write 1 to 2 posts every day to build your content. Without content, search engines have little reason to direct traffic to your site. As I said in Chapter 5, your blog must have a focused theme, which for authors is generally the topic of their book. I have seen some blogs for fiction stories where the author creates a blog for one or several of her fictional characters.

The trick that all of us bloggers want to figure out is how to create content that is interesting enough to keep people coming back, creates word of mouth (visitors telling their friends about our blog), generates comments (both good and bad) and motivates people to link to our blog. Bloggers who talk about news, movies, music, politics etc. achieve this goal fairly easy and if you go to one of these sites you will see a lot of comments. Not all topics will generate a lot of feedback and for some of us we will have to work at it.

For example, after posting for several months on my new blog, I began wondering if there was a way to make my blog more buzz worthy. So I decided to track the promotional campaign of a real author, Diana Derval, on my blog. At the time of this edition, I have just started this experiment so we'll see what happens. You can go to www.howtopublishabookblog.com and see what I'm doing by clicking on the "Live Study—Diana Derval" category on the sidebar.

Another tactic is to start a blog and tie the theme into a popular topic. A great example of this tactic is the www.where-to-now.com blog by Dr. Bill Guillory. Bill blogs about leadership, spirituality and other humanistic topics. He began his blog shortly after Katrina struck and since he was originally from New Orleans and still has family there, Katrina was a topic close to his heart and related to his blog's theme.

Tactic 2: SEO copywriting skills

Tactic 1 talked about writing for people, but when you write on a blog, there are other "tricks of the trade" to use to help the search engines find your content. Chris Conlan, owner of *The Blogmill* and a partner in *Authors on the Net*, allowed me to reprint an article he published on www.ezinearticles.com. Here's his article:

> **SEO Copywriting** is a skill. For most people it's really something you learn over time by doing it, paying close attention to what your competitors are doing and reading up on how to write copy for websites, blogs, press releases and articles.
>
> There are some simple rules that will help the beginning **SEO copywriter** and keep the experienced "know-it-all" like myself grounded!
>
> First let's start by really defining *SEO copywriting*.
>
> SEO copywriting is the art and science of combining three elements:
>
> 1. **Valuable Content:** providing the reader with content that affords them the opportunity to

learn, experience or clarify a product, service, position or opinion. Key factors in creating "value" in your content include organization, a high level of detail, a birds-eye view, reader perspective, usability and specific calls to action.

Your content must provide the reader with "news you can use" if you will. The overall reader experience must take into account a variety of different levels of knowledge/proficiency with the topic. Here's where defining and organizing your thoughts comes in. Start with a bird's eye view of the Who, What, Where, When, Why and How, then expand into greater detail on a point by point or step by step basis.

2. **Readability:** The user must be able to understand what the heck you are talking about. A good rule of thumb is to write for the reader first, then make a second and third pass for the search engines.

3. **Structure and Formatting:** Search Engines are becoming smarter about assessing the "value" of your content, but they still rely on a variety of distinguishable factors which are outlined below. There is no hard and fast rule for any of these tips. Use them all "sparingly" and remember #1 and 2 above.

10 SEO Copywriting Tips
1. **Use Bold, and Italics:** Just like a regular old human reader the search engines give more weight to words and phrases that are in bold or italics. Just don't go too crazy or you'll irritate the *search engines* and give your reader a headache (unless you're selling aspirin, but that's a different article on subliminal copywriting!).

2. **Internal Hyperlinks:** You are your own best resource, so use, and to a certain extent, abuse yourself. Hyperlink to other resources/pages of your site that are relevant to the copy you are writing. This will benefit the reader, increase the amount of time they spend on your site and help you with the search engines.

3. **External Hyperlinks:** Incorporating links to external resources which will benefit the reader can help you in two ways (a) they provide a third-party validation to a certain extent of your "expertise" and (b) afford you the opportunity to pick up some extra coin if that resource provides reciprocal linking or has an affiliate program.

4. **Use Bullet Points:** Using a bullet point or numbered system helps break up your copy into consumable pieces, aids in the clean design of your page and makes it easy for the reader to "go back" and reference previous points without wasting time reading through dense copy.

5. **Content "Mass":** Never have less than 400 words on a page. If the content you are providing is in fact valuable you should be able to come up with around 1,000 words.

6. **Use Examples** to beef up your content with relevant keywords. (See #8).

7. **Keyword Density:** I like to try for 7% density for no more than 4 sets of keywords or phrases per page. Segway to #8.

8. **Break your keyword sets/phrases into tiers or alternates** to enable a better flow while maximizing density and penetration (based upon Yahoo!'s Keyword Selector Tool, WordTracker,

WebCEO or a like keyword recommendation program).

Example: Target: *SEO Copywriting*
Tier 1: **SEO Copywriting**
Tier 2: **SEO Copywriter**
Tier 3: **Writing copy for SEO**
Tier 4: **SEO copywriting services**

Example Sentence: "Instead of spending time evaluating SEO copywriting Services become a SEO copywriter yourself by following these guidelines and you'll be writing copy for SEO in no time."

I sort of packed it all into one sentence, but you should get the gist.

9. **Write for what the reader is searching for, not what you think they should be searching for.** Remember that your job is to provide the "solution" to the problem, not create a greater problem by making the reader/searcher feel dumb. If they are searching for Ham and Green Eggs instead of Green Eggs and Ham, give them Ham and Green Eggs—"The Searcher is Always Right" to paraphrase a service industry mantra.

10. **On Page Structure and Code "Tricks"** There is an old saying from high school debate teams: "Tell them what your gonna tell them, tell them, then tell them what you told them". The same applies to SEO copywriting. Use an "introductory statement", followed by your body content with bullet points or numbering, and then a "summary" (which is essentially the same as your introductory statement). Don't forget to avail yourself of page specific meta tags, page title, ALT Tags, Image Tags, Screen Tips, etc. to fill in the blanks for the words that just didn't

fit into the "flow" and to increase the relevant weight of your selected keywords.

Remember, **SEO Copywriting** is a skill. For most people it's really something you learn over time by doing it, paying close attention to what your competitors are doing and reading up on how to write copy for websites, blogs, press releases and articles.

Kaboodle Ventures SEO Copywriting
The Blog Mill Blog Templates
Article Source: http://EzineArticles.com/
?expert=Christopher_Conlan

While Mr. Conlan's advice is invaluable, a caution I will make is to not let these SEO rules keep you from blogging regularly. It is more important to blog 1 to 2 times a day then to spend a week writing a perfect post for the search engines. I read Chris's 10 tips frequently and try my best to incorporate what he says, but I prioritize getting a blog posted over getting a blog posted with perfect SEO. Over time, I hope to get better.

Tactic 3: Create Links, both Inbound and Outbound

Going back into Sushi Toshi, you'll remember I mentioned that often another patron would give me his business card. This is a "real-world" way to link with people and the natural reaction I make is to link back to him by giving him my business card. When I link to someone on my blog, I am not linking just to get a link back to me, but I am very happy when someone does link back. When you are blogging, it is important to remember that when someone links to you, you really need to consider linking back to that person, unless there is some reason you decide that making a link is not appropriate.

There are several different types of links. One link is when another blogger puts your blog's address in his or her sidebar. This is generally called a blog roll or link roll and when someone puts you on their blogroll this creates an *Inbound* link to your site. Search engines perform better when there are a lot of Inbound links, but the links are more valuable when they are high-quality links. For example, when an author links to my blog about publishing, this creates a high-quality Inbound link because the content on the author's blog will naturally be a good fit for my site and my blog will move up the search engine rankings. However, if a car dealership links to my site, my position on the search engines won't be affected much, if at all.

Another type of link is created when someone mentions you in one of his or her blog posts—a direct link to your site. This is also an Inbound link and again, if the content on the person's blog resembles your content, then this person just gave you a high-quality link. The key point here is that search engines determine which blogs (and websites for that matter) are the most reputable and relevant based on how many other people are linking to that site. Here are a few things to consider when building link relationships:

1. Let the links happen naturally. When someone links to you and their blog is relevant to your content, give that person a link on your blogroll or mention them in one of your posts.

2. Focus on your niche. If you have a book about marketing, then seek out other people who have blogs about marketing. Send them a copy of your book or leave a comment for them on their blogsite.

3. Write articles and submit them to places like www.ezinearticles.com There are thousands of sites where you can post articles you've written, but if you submit your articles to the top 100 then most of the rest of the services feed off these top tier 100 sites. You generate links by posting articles in three ways: (1) When the article website like ezinearticles.com posts your article, an Inbound link is created, (2) when somebody else downloads your article and posts on his or her blog, an Inbound link is created, and (3) if someone reads your article they may visit your site and if they like what they see, they might create a link. This last

one has a lot of ifs, but point three is one way a link can be created to your site.

4. Social Networking, like www.del.icio.us.

5. Leave comments. Whenever I am surfing around and I find a site of interest I will take a few minutes and leave a thoughtful comment. When you leave a comment, you can type in your blog's URL and create a link for your site.

Linking activities to avoid

1. You may find people offering to help you build thousands of links in minutes. Terms these people/companies go by are Link Farms and FFA (Free For All) sites. As with most things in life, good results do not come from "cheating" the system. What you want are good, solid links and not thousands of links from dubious places. I tried this once and ended up with a bunch of pornographic sites on my blogroll. The links were clever as you had to click through a few pages to find the nasty stuff so just a visual inspection of the home page the link took me to did not help me avoid getting a bunch of junk on my blogroll.

2. Webrings: The definition from Wikipedia reads: *A webring in general is a collection of websites from around the Internet joined together in a circular structure. When used to improve search engine rankings, webrings can be considered a search engine optimization technique. To be a part of the webring, each site has a common navigation bar; it contains links to the previous and next site. By clicking next (or previous) repeatedly, the surfer will eventually reach the site they started at; this is the origin of the term webring.*

   Webrings often do not create direct links to your site and with webrings you risk the search engines viewing your webring activity as spam. When I evaluated joining a webring, I chose to spend my time and effort on more substantial social networking activities, primarily writing articles, posting often, leaving good comments and linking with quality sites.

Tactic 4: Collect Email addresses

Once you get people on your blog (into your sales funnel) you want to generate some kind of action. The action authors want is to get people to buy their books or sign up for a seminar or both. But not all visitors will buy a book. Almost as valuable as selling products is to collect a visitor's email address. Here are three ways to encourage visitors to participate more on your blog and share their email addresses with you:

- Customize your "Here's your password" message when visitors register to post or comment.

- Give visitors something free as an incentive for them to register such as a "How to PDF" or a free MP3 download. Include a link to the file in your "Here's Your Password" email.

- Hold a contest, pose a question for the community, or encourage them to voice their opinion.

Tactic 5: Get People Participating and Keep Them Participating

The three bullet points under Tactic 4 are great ways to get people to participate and to share their email addresses with you. Below are ways to generate more participation and to keep people interested in your blog:

- Use a weekly or monthly newsletter to keep them informed.

- Include an "Email This" and "Print This" function on your blog. Let them share the wealth and encourage their friends to register. Build your database.

- Include a Bio Pop Up feature that allows blog "members" to share their personality and background. Dagon Design has a neat plug-in for this one.

- "Partner Up" with a rich media provider such as VoiceAmerica talk radio and add links to rich media content that fits with your blog. For example, if your blog is about health, include links to their website, or ask them if they have a popup player that you could add as a rich media feature to your blog. This begins to make your blog a cross media destination as opposed to just something visitors can read.

- Add a tracking feature for your users to be able to follow other users comments on a specific topic or posting. Again Dagon Design has a great plug-in for this one. (Aside— you can get all these free plug-ins at http://www-blog-template-layout.com)

Tactic 6: Keep the Spam off your Blog

Once your blog is off and running, pinging out of control and people are participating, it's important to keep the spam off your blog. Nothing is more annoying to the user than having to sift through non-appropriate content. Dealing with articles and postings "Awaiting Moderation" can become cumbersome, so try to "nip it in the bud" when it comes to every Romanian or Indonesian blog spammer that comes along. If you're using WordPress the Askimet plug-in works great, it comes with the free 2.0 download, but you'll need a WordPress API code (free).

When I first started blogging, I would scan through my spam—about 50 per day—to see if any legitimate comments were identified as spam. I found none and so after about 3 months of testing the Askimet spam plug in I now feel confident enough to just hit the Delete All button. On the other hand, I often get spam sneaking through to my comments and this is annoying, but still it is easy to identify the spam and just delete them. Spam is one of the annoying evils of the net, but luckily there are tools to help us manage spam's negative effects.

Tactic 7: Make Sure Your Bloggers Can Contact You

Don't expect everyone of your readers or group to want to post their "personal" comment on your blog. Some people actually still do value their privacy! Make sure there is an easy way for them to contact you directly, especially if you're answering questions or hoping that someone will ask you for a custom proposal. One more time Dagon Design has a great plug-in for a Contact Form (Formmailer) and it has a visual security code that keeps the spammers away. It's easy to configure, free and comes ready for WordPress and in a standalone PHP format if you use another blog program.

Tactic 8: Incorporate Your Existing Site

Regardless of whether you're running a standalone blog or running one connected to your main site, make sure you include hard static links back to your order form, about us, product white papers, contact information, etc. in your blog. It's not hard to do, put it in the Links section, or add direct links in your header and/or footer. Most blogging software isn't really ready for shopping carts (although there are some plugins out there in Beta that look promising) but that doesn't mean you can't have one. With a little creativity in your header, footer and sidebar you can utilize all of the functionality you currently have on your website, or anyone else's website.

Are you feeling a little overwhelmed? Don't get too discouraged because the good news is that you don't have to do everything yourself. Authors On The Net offers some great low-cost solutions that can help you do all the SEO you will need to get up and running. Besides being an author Mastermind community, AON is designed to be an action center; a place where you can build and manage your promotional plan. We built AON so an author can learn how to promote on the internet himself or herself or to use third-party vendors. But even if you are going to pay other people to help you, we hope the learning center, along with this book, will arm you with enough information to know what you want. In other words, our goal is to give authors enough information to either do what they want themselves or get what they want done without losing their shirts.

Before we move on to Chapter Seven where I'll introduce some other "DRILL BITS," we need to cover the topics of pinging and RSS or Really Simple Syndication.

Tactic 9: Pinging

Pinging is the act of letting search engines know you have just created new content on your blog. Before loading the automatic ping function into my blog, I would go to ping-o-matic.com and manually ping the search engines each time I created new content. While this step was fast and easy, it was still another action item I had to do each day. With the plugin, I don't even think about pinging anymore.

The plugin is at http://wp-plugins.net/ as are most other Wordpress plugins. If you choose to have someone else build your Wordpress blog, be sure to have them include this function.

Tactic 10: Really Simple Syndication—RSS

This section is going to explain what RSS is and why this code has revolutionized how we communicate. Understanding the details of RSS is not as important as understanding how to make RSS work for you. Let's begin with the Wikipedia definition:

RSS is a family of web feed formats used to publish frequently updated digital content, such as blogs, news feeds or podcasts. Users of RSS content use software programs called "feed readers" or "feed aggregators." The user subscribes to a feed by entering a link of the feed into the reader program. The reader can then check the user's subscribed feeds to see if any of those feeds have new content since the last time it was checked, and, if so, retrieve that content and present it to the user.

The initials "RSS" are variously used to refer to the following standards:

- *Really Simple Syndication (RSS 2.0)*
- *Rich Site Summary (RSS 0.91, RSS 1.0)*
- *RDF Site Summary (RSS 0.9 and 1.0)*

RSS formats are specified in XML (a generic specification for data formats). RSS delivers its information as an XML file called an "RSS feed," "webfeed," "RSS stream," or "RSS channel."

An aggregator or news aggregator or feed reader is a client software that uses web feed to retrieve syndicated web content such as blogs, podcasts, vlogs, and mainstream mass media websites, or in the case of a search aggregator, a customized set of search results.

A web feed is a data format used for serving users frequently updated content. Content distributors syndicate a web feed, thereby allowing users to subscribe to it. Making a collection of web feeds accessible in one spot is known as aggregation.

In the typical scenario of using web feeds, a content provider publishes a feed link on their site which end users can register with an aggregator program (also called a feed reader or a news reader) running on their own machines; doing this is usually as simple as dragging the link from the web browser to the aggregator. When instructed, the aggregator asks all the servers in its feed list if they have new content; if so, the aggregator either makes a note of the new content or downloads it. Aggregators can be scheduled to check for new content periodically.

The kinds of content delivered by a web feed are typically HTML (webpage content) or links to webpages and other kinds of digital media. Often when websites provide web feeds to notify users of content updates, they only include summaries in the web feed rather than the full content itself. Many news web sites, weblogs, schools, and podcasters operate web feeds.

Again, understanding these technical terms is not as important as knowing how to use the RSS tools. The main reason Blogs are gaining in popularity is that RSS code allows you to syndicate your writing. Syndicating your writing simply means that people can subscribe to your content and every time you write something new, your information will download automatically to your reader's computer.

The three key points about RSS feeds are: 1. Make sure your blog is equipped with RSS feeds to allow visitors to subscribe to receive your information, 2. Put the feed reader of your choice on your computer and 3. Know how to copy and paste RSS code from Blogs you like into your reader. To find out more, you can subscribe to www.AuthorsOnTheNet.com and watch the instructional videos.

When I first started blogging it took me three weeks to understand RSS and how to use my feedreader effectively. The concept is not difficult, but the videos will save you time if you are new to feedreaders. I currently use my feedreader to keep track of 20 blogs I want to socialize with and we'll talk more about how to use this tool in the next chapters.

7

More DRILL Bits

• • •

I took a speed-reading course and read 'War and Peace' in twenty minutes. It involves Russia.
– WOODY ALLEN

When I was first contemplating this book, I wanted to include every Internet tactic known to humankind. This first idea had at least four problems:

- The book would have been longer than *'War and Peace'* and not nearly as entertaining.

- The book would have been so full of tactics it would have created that 'noise' effect Sun Tzu spoke about.

- As the Internet changes daily, by the time this book was actually read by someone, there might be 50 more tactics readers can use.

- Readers would have a hard time choosing which tactics to use without an overall strategic plan

As this book goes hand-in-hand with the Authors On The Net website, I was able to focus on some of the top-level tactics authors should first focus their attention on. For example, becoming an expert Amazon user, learning how to effectively blog and other tactics. The AON website allows us to keep the Internet tactics and tools fresh and relevant for authors who subscribe to the service.

However, as not every reader of *DRILL* will subscribe to the AON website, I will introduce some of the key tactics authors can use to promote their books online. The tactics I have chosen to introduce should be with us a while.

The approach I recommend with these tactics is to first read through them to get an overview of what they are and make notes on whether you might want to include a tactic in your plan. While it may only take you a few minutes to read this chapter, implementing each tactic might take days, weeks or even months. One reason making a plan is important is to layout each tactic you want to use and to take the necessary time to implement it correctly. While many of these online tactics can be implemented fast and furiously, the execution of the tactics is something that needs to be done on a daily basis for as long as you decide to dig for your treasure.

Book Trailers

A **book trailer** is a video advertisement for a book which employs techniques similar to those of movie trailers. They are circulated online in most common digital video formats. The term "Book Trailer" is trademarked by Circle of Seven Productions. If you want to see some examples of Book Trailers you can go to www.authorsonthenet.com and watch videos we've placed in the "Author Tools" section. You can also go to YouTube and search for "Book Trailers" to see many samples.

The cost for a Book Trailer ranges from $250 to $50,000. After the Book Trailer is created, the video needs to be distributed. Sample places to distribute your Book Trailer include:

- Online Social Sites (MySpace, YouTube, Yahoo, Grouper, MSN, and Google)

- Booksellers

- Publishers

- Online Magazines

Here's a small excerpt from Newsweek about Book Trailers titled, *Trailers: Seen Any Good Books Lately. To read the entire article, click here: http://www.msnbc.msn.com/id/12776738/site/newsweek/*

May 22, 2006 issue—Publishers and authors are increasingly commissioning trailers for books . . . that can be viewed on their Web sites and even aired on TV and in movie theaters. "We've seen a huge increase in interest [for book trailers]," says Sheila Clover, whose company, Circle of Seven Productions, pioneered the concept in 2002 and has trademarked the term "book trailer."

Conventional wisdom has long been that viewers aren't readers—and vice versa. But as bloggers and media outlets have shown the popularity of blending print with multimedia online, booksellers are now jumping onboard. "We love this concept," says Bantam Dell's Caroline Schwartz. "Because books are entertainment, too." Even if it takes a movie to remind us of that.

– Elise Soukup
© 2006 Newsweek, Inc.

Two sites you can visit directly to learn more about book trailers are:

http://www.cosproductions.com/
http://www.bookshorts.com/

A book trailer gives you another tool to put on the web for people to learn about your book. Hundreds, if not thousands of people will view your book trailer and be directed to your blog or other online book store to make a purchase.

Depending on how interesting you make your trailer, people may start putting your trailer on their own blog sites. I have loaded up several book trailers on my blog because they are related to my theme—book promotion, I want to give free publicity to authors who have visited my site and having these trailers helps bring people to my own blog. If I am willing to put book trailers on my site, how many other people might be willing to put your trailer on their site? Once your book trailer is on YouTube, people all over the world can link to your trailer, a step that takes less than a minute.

Virtual Book Tours

There are two types of Virtual Book Tours, the tele-seminar model and the blog site visit model. The tele-seminar model is when you set up a tele-seminar and attract as many people as possible to dial in to a phone conference and listen to you talk about your book in-depth. Usually, someone else will interview authors during the tele-seminar to make the interview more interesting. Another tactic authors will use is that prior to holding the tele-seminar they will run an "Ask" campaign, which is a way to collect questions from real readers about the author's book. The author will then address these questions during the tele-seminar.

The second type of VBT is when the author sets up a number of visits to other people's blog sites. The owner of the Blog lets customers know the author will be visiting and during the visit the author will usually:

- Be interviewed by the site's owner or someone else
- Make Blog entries
- Answer questions from Blog visitors
- Submit their book for review
- Give away digital copies

You can find out more about Tele-seminar VBTs by going to the book promotion section on AON (www.authorsonthenet.com) and you can find vendors ready to help you by visiting the partners section.

If you are not a member of AON, three sites you can visit to find out more are:

http://www.alexmandossian.com/
http://www.kevinsmokler.com/virtual_book_tour.html
http://thedabblingmum.com/writing/hostevent/blogtour.htm

Podcasting

A podcast is a digital media file, or a series of such files, that is distributed over the Internet using syndication feeds for playback on portable media players and personal computers. A podcast is a specific type of webcast, which, like 'radio', can mean either the content itself or the method by which it is syndicated; the latter is also termed podcasting. The host or author of a podcast is often called a podcaster. The term "podcast" combines the name of Apple's portable music player, the iPod, and broadcast; a "pod" refers to a container of some sort, and "cast" to the idea of broadcasting.

In other words, a podcast is a collection of files (usually audio and video) residing at a unique web feed address. People can "subscribe' to this feed by submitting the feed address to an aggregator (like iTunes). When new "episodes" become available in the podcast they will be automatically downloaded to that users computer. Unlike radio, or streaming content on the web podcasts are not real-time. There is no live broadcast of content, the material is pre-recorded and users can check out the material at their leisure, offline.

Though podcasters' web sites may also offer direct download or streaming of their content, a podcast is distinguished from other digital media formats by its ability to be syndicated, subscribed to, and downloaded automatically, using an aggregator or feed reader capable of reading feed formats such as RSS or Atom.

Podcasting is increasing in popularity. According to Forrester Research, by 2010 podcasting should have about 12.3 million listeners. That's a pretty big audience. For more info see http://tinyurl.com/84tyo (http://en.wikipedia.org/wiki/Podcasting)

A Podcast can be just about anything you want it to be. For authors, a popular Podcast format is to be interviewed. For business coaches and other non-fiction books, hosting your own Podcast once a week or every two weeks is also a good strategy. Like blogging, you need to Podcast on a regular basis so listeners will subscribe to your feed and consequently begin building your database of potential customers.

There is no rule for the length of a Podcast, but you generally want to keep them less than 30 minutes. If you have an hour-long recording, that's fine, simply break it into two parts of 30 minutes each or 4 parts of 15 minutes each. A one-hour audio clip broken into 4 parts will give you a month's worth of material. Short clips done often are better than a long clip done once.

The physical part of creating a Podcast is the easy part. Coming up with creative and interesting content will be difficult for many people. Some people are gifted entertainers and will thrive in the Podcast environment. As with Blogging, you need to have a theme and stick to the theme because that is what people will be subscribing to. If your first five episodes are about raising cats and then with your sixth episode you begin to talk about how to make horror movies, you'll lose your crowd. Start a new Podcast channel for each topic you want to talk about. Also, when you get started you may feel uncomfortable. One of the reasons for that is in the beginning you are finding your voice. The best advice is to listen to many Podcasts in your genre before you begin your own. This will give you an idea of how others talk on their Podcasts.

The actual mechanics of creating your Podcast are:

1. Get software to record your own audio file. A good free one is Audacity, which you can download at http://audacity.sourceforge.net/

   While there, you'll also need to download the Lame MP3 Encoder, which allows MP3 exportation.

   You'll also need a recorder. You can buy inexpensive digital recorders at many outlets. I bought mine at Best Buy for $179.00. These recorders are small, but they produce sound quality good enough for Podcasts and they are easy to use.

2. Once your audio is recorded you'll need to create an RSS feed file, which is simply a special text file with an RSS extension that also includes a particular enclosure tag. For step-by-step directions on making a feed file see this site:

   http://make-rss-feeds.com/making-an-rss-feed.htm

There's also a great tutorial on RSS here: http://www.mnot.net/rss/tutorial/

3. Once your audio and RSS files are completed, you'll need to upload both of them to your server/website. Here are some online sites to help guide you.

- Make Your First Podcast http://tinyurl.com/757fx

- Create Podcasts Using Your PC http://tinyurl.com/9jfcb

If you don't want to do all this work manually there are software tools specific to podcast creation.

- FeedForAll http://www.feedforall.com/podcasting-tutorial.htm

- ePodCast Creator http://tinyurl.com/do7sq

- Pod Producer http://tinyurl.com/9dwrh

Remember, you can't get subscribers if people don't know about your feed, so make sure you add the feed in a prominent place on your site. You want to make it easy for visitors to subscribe and add your feed to their newsreader.

Online press releases

Online press releases are the same as standard press releases, the difference being the method of distribution. Wikipedia defines a press release as follows:

A news release, press release or press statement is a written or recorded communication directed at members of the news media for the purpose of announcing something claimed as having news value. Typically, it is mailed, faxed, or e-mailed to assignment editors at newspapers, magazines, radio stations, television stations, and/or television networks. Commercial press-release distribution services such as Eworldwire are also used to distribute news releases. Sometimes news releases are sent for the purpose of announcing news conferences.

A news release is different from a news article. A news article is a compilation of facts developed by journalists published in the news media, whereas a news release is sent to journalists to encourage them to develop articles on the subject. A news release is generally biased towards the objectives of the author.

The use of news releases is common in the field of public relations, the aim of which is to attract favorable media attention to the PR firm's client, and publicity, the aim of which is to attract favorable media attention for products marketed by the client.

Writing an online press release follows the same rules as a standard press release. One of the most common services for online press releases is PR Web Direct, www.prwebdirect.com. Here's a blurb from PR Web Direct's website:

> PRWeb® distributes press releases for many Fortune 500 companies and is the largest Newswire catering to small and medium-sized companies and organizations. PRWeb® currently stands as one of the largest overall online press release newswires anywhere.
>
> In 1997, PRWeb® pioneered a new method for online press release distribution. This inventive method met the growing need to accomplish two fundamental objectives. PRWeb observed that the increasing volume of press releases made it impossible for the media to follow up on every story. We needed to develop a system to bypass this 'media bottleneck' by placing your stories directly in front of your target audience. In addition, your message needed to be expressly communicated to the media. We made it our mission to meet these two challenges. We have spent thousands of man-hours developing our state of the art distribution engine to get your stories placed with the media and more importantly in front of your audience.

PR Web is just one service available to anyone to submit an online press release. The fees vary, but are relatively low-cost and the staff at PR Web can help you draft and optimize your release.

On the following page is an example of a real press release by author Bill Ferguson, author of *'Miracles are Guaranteed.'*

Broken New Year's Resolutions—How to Fix Them

Author, counselor and Oprah guest Bill Ferguson offers advice for salvaging those abandoned New Years resolutions and making real changes in your life.

(PRWEB via <u>IdeaLady</u>) February 7, 2006—With the New Year, millions of people make resolutions about their health, their work and their relationships. Within weeks, the resolutions have been broken and the people who made them are left feeling like failures. Making changes with superficial resolutions doesn't work, says author and counselor Bill Ferguson. To change your life, start from the inside. These seven steps, adapted from his new book, Miracles are Guaranteed (available in bookstores and at <u>http://www.MasteryOfLife.com/</u>) will help anyone create a life that works.

- Be positive. The words you speak and the thoughts you accept determine how you view life. You then act consistent with the way you view life and life proves your point of view to be true. If you want a life that works, don't speak negatively or accept negative thoughts about yourself, other people or your life.

- Accept yourself. You are the way you are whether you like it or not. Until you make peace with the way you are, you will never make peace with life. Accept every aspect of yourself, particularly the aspects that you don't like.

- Let go. When you resist the way life is, you get upset and lose your ability to see clearly. You destroy love and make your situation worse. To restore both your effectiveness and your peace of mind, let go of your demands for how life should be and flow with the way life is. Then take whatever action you need to have your life be great.

- Accept full responsibility for your life. When you accept full 100% responsibility for what happens in your life, you have power. Others may also be responsible, but when you blame other people, they get your power. You become a victim and unable to take effective action. When you accept responsibility, you get your power back.

- Don't overspend. Upsets about money seem to be due to a lack of income, but this is seldom the case. Money upsets are almost always due to over-spending. When spending exceeds your income, you can expect to get upset. To create a life of prosperity, make sure you spend less than you make and appreciate what you have.

- Find a dream to go for. When you have a dream to go for, life becomes an exciting adventure. You have direction and a reason for living. You add spice to your life. If you don't have a dream to go for, get one as fast as you can.

- Serve. Have your life be about more than you. When you put focus on yourself, upsets and problems grow. When you focus on serving, upsets and problems dissolve. Find something more important than you and throw yourself into it.

- Bill's free Mastery of Life e-course shows how to clear up the areas of your life that are not working. It is available at http://www.MasteryOfLife.com/ Bill Ferguson spent most of his adult life studying the nature of love. He discovered that whenever love is present, life works. You are happy, alive and free. You radiate a very positive energy and great things happen. By creating this experience of love, you create a life that works.

Bill has been recommended by The Wall Street Journal and featured in newspapers, magazines, and on radio and television talk shows across the country, including Oprah. Bill Ferguson is available for interview. For more information, call 713-520-5370 or visit Bill on the Web at http://www.MasteryOfLife.com and http://www.DivorceAsFriends.com

Contact Info:
Bill Ferguson
Mastery of Life Seminars
http://www.MasteryOfLife.com/
713-520-5370

You can also hire a PR firm to assist you, but most firms will charge thousands of dollars for their services. Using a PR firm makes sense only if you estimate the return justifies the investment. For example, if a PR firm will charge you $5,000 and you make on average $3.00 per book, then you will need to sell 1,670 books to get your money back. For most authors, making a return on a $5,000 press kit will be difficult. But if you also sell consulting services (like Bill Ferguson in our example above), then spending $5,000 may be a good marketing tactic. PR Web is a low-cost way to send out press releases and fits nearly every budget.

Book Reviews

The value of an objective book review is priceless in your battle to gain word-of-mouth exposure. A book review is a critical appraisal of a book that evaluates a book based on its writing style, its market appeal and what importance it might play in a cultural, political or literary aspect. Here's a sample book review from the New York Times:

A Thousand Splendid Suns
By Michiko Kakutani
May 29, 2007

It's not that hard to understand why Khaled Hosseini's first novel, "The Kite Runner" (2003), became such a huge best seller, based largely on word of mouth and its popularity among book clubs and reading groups. The novel read like a kind of modern-day variation on Conrad's "Lord Jim," in which the hero spends his life atoning for an act of cowardice and betrayal committed in his youth. It not only gave readers an intimate look at Afghanistan and the difficulties of life there, but it also showed off its author's accessible and very old-fashioned storytelling talents: his taste for melodramatic plotlines; sharply drawn,

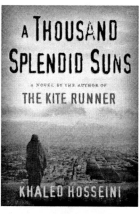

"A Thousand Splendid Suns" by Khaled Hosseini

black-and-white characters; and elemental boldfaced emotions.

Whereas "The Kite Runner" focused on fathers and sons, and friendships between men, his latest novel, "A Thousand Splendid Suns," focuses on mothers and daughters, and friendships between women. Whereas "Kite Runner" got off to a gripping start and stumbled into contrivance and sentimentality in its second half, "Splendid Suns" starts off programmatically and gains speed and emotional power as it slowly unfurls.

Like its predecessor, the new novel features a very villainous villain and an almost saintly best friend who commits an act of enormous self-sacrifice to aid the hero/heroine. Like its predecessor, it attempts to show the fallout that Afghanistan's violent history has had on a handful of individuals, ending in death at the hands of the Taliban for one character, and the promise of a new life for another. And like its predecessor, it features some embarrassingly hokey scenes that feel as if they were lifted from a B movie, and some genuinely heart-wrenching scenes that help redeem the overall story.

Mr. Hosseini, who was born in Kabul and moved to the United States in 1980, writes in straight-ahead, utilitarian prose and creates characters that have the simplicity and primary-colored emotions of people in a fairy tale or fable. The sympathy he conjures for them stems less from their personalities (the hero of "Kite Runner" was an unlikable coward who failed to come to the aid of his best friend) than from the circumstances in which they find themselves: contending with un-happy families, abusive marriages, oppressive govern-ments and repressive cultural mores.

In the case of "Splendid Suns," Mr. Hosseini quickly makes it clear that he intends to deal with the plight of women in Afghanistan, and in the opening pages the mother of one of the novel's two heroines talks porten-tously about "our lot in life," the lot of poor, uned-ucated "women like us" who have to endure the hard-ships of life, the slights of men, the disdain of society.

This heavy-handed opening quickly gives way to even more "soap operaish" events: after her mother commits suicide, the teenage Mariam—the illegitimate daughter of a wealthy man, who is ashamed of her ex-istence—is quickly married off to a much older shoe-maker named Rasheed, a piggy brute of a man who says it embarrasses him "to see a man who's lost control of his wife."

Rasheed forces Mariam to wear a burka and treats her with ill-disguised contempt, subjecting her to scorn, ridicule, insults, even "walking past her like she was nothing but a house cat." Mariam lives in fear of "his shifting moods, his volatile temperament, his insistence on steering even mundane exchanges down a confron-tational path that, on occasion, he would resolve with punches, slaps, kicks, and sometimes try to make amends for with polluted apologies and sometimes not."

The life of the novel's other heroine, Lila, who becomes Rasheed's second wife, takes an even sharper trajectory toward ruin. Though she is the cherished daughter of an intellectual, who encourages her to pursue an education, Lila finds her life literally shattered when a rocket—lobbed by one of the warlord factions fighting for control of Kabul, after the Soviet Union's departure—lands on her house and kills her parents.

Her beloved boyfriend, Tariq, has already left Kabul with his family—they have become refugees in Pakistan—and she suddenly finds that she is an orphan with no resources or friends. When she discovers that she is pregnant with Tariq's child and learns that Tariq has supposedly died from injuries sustained in a rocket attack near the Pakistan border, she agrees to marry Rasheed, convinced that she and her baby will never survive alone on the streets of Kabul.

There are literally thousands of places you can get your book reviewed, from local niche papers and radio stations to larger local papers to national papers like the New York Times to a myriad of online services. Most services have a submission process to follow. The key point is that for just about any book, there is a place where you can have it reviewed.

We have an author at ZDocs who wrote a unique book titled *Death and Dying in Park City Utah*. His book is a collection of short obituaries of people who died during a certain period of history in Park City, Utah. Gary Kimball, the author, had his book reviewed in a couple of local newspapers and the local NPR station interviewed him. Gary sold over 1,000 copies of his book, a huge success story for a book that really had no genre.

Some great places to start submitting your book for reviews are:

> http://www.thebookreviewersite.com
> www.simegen.com/reviews/
> http://www.scribesworld.com/index.html
> http://www.ivyquill.com
> http://www.romrevtoday.com/general_fiction_-_june.htm

http://www.simplydreams.net
http://www.wordweaving.com

This list is only a representation of what you can find online. While you will want to tap into your local media, as Gary Kimball did, to find the niche magazines and newspapers that will give you an honest review, you will also want to scan the web to find places that will review your book. A book review is a marketing tool you can use in all of your promotional activities.

Another type of book review is a paid review. A paid review should be a critical review of your work that gives you insight into how to appeal to your target audience more effectively or how to write your book more professionally. For example, you can go to http://www.writefieldservices.com/critiqueservices.html and pay $305.00 for a book review.

Social Networks

The first social network website was Classmates.com, which began in 1995. Other sites followed, including SixDegrees.com, which began in 1997 using the Web of Contacts model. The year 1999 saw the development of two competing models of social networking, the Circle of Trust developed by Epinions and utilized by Ciao.com, Dooyoo and ToLuna and the Circle of Friends developed by Jonathan Bishop, which was utilized on a number of regional UK sites between 1999 and 2001 and flourished with the advent of a website called Friendster in 2002. This is now one of the most dominant methods of social networking in virtual communities, perhaps for the reason that it gives the user control rather than being computer controlled.

There were over 50 social networking sites using the Circle of Friends in 2005 when one such online community, MySpace, was getting more page views than Google. Google has a social network called Orkut, launched in 2004. Social networking began to be seen as a component of Internet strategy at around the same time. In March 2005, Yahoo launched Yahoo! 360°, their entry into the field, and in July 2005 News Corporation bought Circle of Friends-based

MySpace, followed by ITV buying Old Boy Network-based Friends Reunited in December that year. It is estimated that combined there are now over 200 social networking sites using these existing and emerging social networking models.

In these communities, an initial set of founders sends out messages inviting members of their own personal networks to join the site. New members repeat the process, growing the total number of members and links in the network. Sites then offer features such as automatic address book updates, viewable profiles, the ability to form new links through "introduction services," and other forms of online social connections. Social networks can also be organized around business connections, as in the case of LinkedIn.

Blended networking is an approach to social networking that combines both offline elements (face-to-face events) and online elements. MySpace, for example, builds on independent music and party scenes, and Facebook was originally designed to mirror a college community, though it has since expanded its scope to include high school, job-related, and regional networks. The newest social networks on the Internet are becoming more focused on niches such as travel, art, tennis, football (soccer), golf, cars, dog owners, and even cosmetic surgery. Other social networking sites focus on local communities, sharing local business and entertainment reviews, news, event calendars and happenings.

There are many discussions as to where social networking is headed next. The advent of the Internet has enabled informal social networks to connect with people globally and with time shifting (through email), although in practice, most interactions are with people who live and work nearby.

A new type of social network is links between web pages. These can be studied in their own right and as links between individual's web pages in social software where individuals begin with their address book, and expand their network by adding friends, "friendster" acquaintances and imaginary friends. This creates connectivity through being discovered through friends of friends, etc. Future applications may allow for discovering the social networks of others by stumbling upon them.

http://en.wikipedia.org/wiki/Social_networking

Authors On The Net is a social network for authors where authors can interact with each other and participate in the community. In addition to the community, however, we have also created a mastermind service that helps authors create a promotional plan and then execute that plan. We envision authors connecting with other authors and learning together to become better at selling books.

Here's a short list of communities discussed in the Wikipedia excerpt above and others not listed but quickly becoming vital communities to participate in.

> www.classmates.com
> www.friendster.com
> www.myspace.com
> www.orkut.com
> http://360.yahoo.com
>> (the site says it's still in beta test, but I've noticed that Yahoo runs their beta tests for years. Not sure why.)
> www.facebook.com
> www.secondlife.com
> www.netscape.com
> www.digg.com
> http://del.icio.us
> http://ma.gnolia.com
> www.stumbleupon.com
> www.authorsonthenet.com

I imagine there are people who participate in all of these and other groups and each author will need to "invent" his/her own strategy for engaging in social networking. I recommend authors spend time looking at the sites listed above (and others you may find) and develop a strategy. For example, classmates.com and friendster.com are different types of communities than secondlife.com and magnolia.com. You can use classmates.com to let your former classmates know you've just published a book. You can participate on magnolia.com to connect with new people. You can use netscape.com to post articles and drive people to your blog.

How you choose to use these communities, if you choose to use them at all, is a decision only you can make based on your overall plan, your resources and, most importantly, your time. For example, if selling books is a primary source of income for you, you may want to devote several hours a day to networking activities. On the other hand, if you have limited time, but a nice bank account, you might hire college students (or your own children) to manage some of your networking activities.

When networking, keep in mind the purpose of your networking. Your end goal is to sell books, but in order to sell books, you need to create a grass-roots buzz about your book. You need word-of-mouth and if you are successful in your efforts, your book will go viral, which means the word about your book begins to spread around the net like a wildfire.

When you begin your social networking activities, keep in mind the man digging for his treasure and Sun Tzu's quote about opportunities multiplying as there are seized. Every time you interact on a social network or on someone else's blog, that interaction (an article, a comment etc.) stays on the site. The more interaction you conduct, the more "opportunities" you offer someone to find out about your book.

Here's an example of what I mean. One day a high school student from New Jersey sent me an email. She said that she read a comment on "someone's" blog that ZDocs was a good place to self-publish. I don't know what comment she read or who wrote the comment and neither does she. But somewhere out on the Internet is a nice comment about ZDocs left by someone who thought it would be helpful to mention my company.

While posting content everyday to your blog is critical, you will begin to see real traffic to your blog—the kind of traffic you want—when you begin to interact with others through social networks and commenting on other blogs.

Email campaigns

Your first email campaign should be to a list of people in your inner circle. Start listing up all the people you know from high school, college, work, church and other groups. Classmates.com and other social networks can help you build your list. Your Blog will also be a source for new contacts and you can use companies to help you expand your list.

A simple Google search using the key words "effective email campaigns" will deliver millions of companies willing to help you run your campaign. Another email strategy is to find partners who have lists of people that might be interested in your book. Ask your partner to send out a message about your book and in return you will send out a message to your group that benefits your friend.

According to the latest Forrester Research numbers, the permission based e-mail industry is projected to grow from $164M (USD) in 1999 to $7.3B by 2005, becoming one of the largest avenues for companies to get their message out to customers. The dark side of email campaigns is, of course, spam. Spamming is not an activity I would ever want to participate in. But developing a solid list of people interested in what I have to offer them is an activity I would invest my time and money into.

The key is quality. You want a quality list of people who have "opted-in" to receive emails from you. How to run an effective email campaign is a topic for another book, but here are a few hints to get you pointed in the right direction:

1. Permission-based email, also called Opt-in email, is established when a person agrees to let a company send them email. Once on the list, if a person wants to "Opt-out" he or she can by simply clicking on a link in the email. Email solicitations are regulated by legislation.

2. The company you choose to help you should have extensive experience in running email campaigns. The company should know how to write ads in the subject line and how to effectively write the first few lines, as most people will not read much further unless the ad gets their attention. Another decision will be to use graphics or text in the ad. Consumers tend to prefer graphics; business customers tend to prefer text ads.

3. Costs can vary from .05 cents per email to .25 cents per email. As there is many choices, shop around, but keep in mind, the higher-priced companies may deliver better results.

4. As with any advertising campaign, the response rate is one way to evaluate how successful the campaign is. Response rates vary from 4% to 20%, which is a pretty wide gap. Looking at the numbers is important. If you have a 20% response rate, but don't sell any books, then your email campaign is effective, but there is some other reason your book isn't selling. It could be your website is poorly designed or that people aren't finding your book interesting. On the other hand, if you have a 2% response rate, then your email campaign isn't as effective as it could be.

5. Most campaigns will create several messages and send out small test samples to see which ad is most effective.

6. Most ad campaigns should direct people to a "landing page" which looks a lot like a webpage but is specific to the action you want your visitors to take, like buy your book. A landing page does not have menu buttons to navigate people off the page. A landing page should close sales.

7. The company you choose to work with should provide tracking reports to evaluate the effectiveness of your campaign and provide insight for future campaigns.

8. As with blogs, email marketing is also a soft sell. Because email is inexpensive, marketers can afford to sell more indirectly. A good approach is to try to create interactivity with your market. Encourage them to visit your landing page or blog site. What approach you use depends on your book, but the point is to think "soft" sell and to make your messages engaging.

9. A truly effective campaign is one that is customized to its target audience. Spam is generally messages sent to people not interested in the product. An effective campaign will target ideal customers.

10. The way to create great lists is to focus on quality rather than quantity. On your web page or in your email blast, let the reader choose the information he or she wants. For example, click here to get the latest installment of my book on how to cook outdoors. This creates value and generates a list of people actually interested in getting that kind of information.

11. Messages should be short and sweet. Images are useful but should be easy to load (under 80Kbps). People will spend just seconds evaluating your message. If they are interested, they'll read on, but not for long. The key is to create an action that moves a customer along your sales funnel.

12. E-mail is a one-way medium, but it still can be made dynamic. Monster.com, for example, sends salary calculators to recipients and Procter & Gamble's HomeMade Simple newsletter incorporates surveys to keep subscribers engaged. Even a "click here" link is better than a static message.

Listings

This tactic is all about trying to "force" your book to go viral and is an important digging tool. Most authors know they need to place their book on Amazon, but few know or take the time to list their book everywhere possible. The following list introduces many places where you can list your book. As the Internet is always changing with services coming and going, some of these places may not exist when you try to visit them. In addition, you may not want to place your book on some or many of these sites. But if you find a handful of other places to list your book, you are increasing your chances of getting your book to go viral.

http://apage4you.com/
http://dmoz.org/
http://ebooks.searchking.com/
http://ebooksrock.net/
http://epublishingnetwork.com/

http://members.aol.com/ebookpromo/
   Author_Directory.htm
http://publishing.about.com/
http://theebookcatalog.webvena.com/listing.html
http://url0.com/ebooks/addsite.html
http://writersonthe.net/
http://www.ala.org/par
http://www.ala.org/parentspage/greatsites/
   sitesug.html
http://www.allreaders.com/
http://www.authorfind.com/
http://www.authorspage.com/
http://www.bitbooks.com/
http://www.bookzen.com/
http://www.cabinfeverbooksearch.com/
http://www.catharton.com/authors/add.htm
http://www.claytabletpublishing.com/
http://www.duckquacks.com/Links.htm
   (for childrens books)
http://www.ebookad.com/
http://www.ebookbroadcast.com/
http://www.ebookcafe.com/
http://www.ebookfriends.com/
http://www.ebookhome.com/
http://www.ebookjungle.com/
http://www.ebookpalace.com/
http://www.ebooksnbytes.com/
http://www.ePubbed.com/
http://www.epublishingnetwork.com/
http://www.escapetoromance.com/author
http://www.greatromancenovels.com/
http://www.kdhbooks.com
http://www.knowbetter.com/
http://www.mind-like-water.com/
http://www.published.com/
http://www.readersanonymous.com/

http://www.romanticnotions.com/
http://www.slake.com/
http://www.specficworld.com/
http://www.stephenjwilliams.co.uk/
http://www.thesavvyclick.com/
http://www.writers-exchange.com/
http://www.writers.net/
http://www.xenite.org/internet_authors/
    internet_authors

Entering your book in contests

Winning an award in a book contest will give you a great PR piece. It will also build credibility for your book and you as an author—especially for writers of fiction. While you will want to look into any local writing contests, the Internet offers you many more options. Here is a list of some you can look in to.

Canadian Science Fiction and Fantasy Association
http://www.sentex.net/~dmullin/aurora/

The Booker McConnel Prize
http://ncc1701.apana.org.au/~larrik...zes/booker.html

John W. Campbell Award
http://www.sff.net/campbell-awards/Winners.htm

Canada's Major National Literary Awards
http://www.nlc-bnc.ca/services/quickref/elitawar.htm

Compton Crook Award
http://www.bsfs.org/bsfsccw.htm

The Darrell Awards
http://members.aol.com/memphen/darrell.htm

Ditmars
http://home.vicnet.net.au/~sfoz/dityear.htm

The Endeavor Award
http://www.osfci.org/endeavour/index.html

European SF Award
http://homepage.tinet.ie/~goudriaan...ml#anchor108182

Joan Fassler Award
http://dpsinfo.com/awardweb/fassler.html

Firecracker Alternative Book Award
http://www.thecomicstore.com/Merchant/fabawards.htm

The Miles Franklin Award
http://ncc1701.apana.org.au/~larrik...s/milesfkn.html

French SF Awards (in French)
http://www.quarante-deux.org/prix_litteraires_sf.html

Jack Gaughan Award for Best Emerging Artist
http://www.nesfa.org/gaughan.html

Hugo Awards (info only)
http://dpsinfo.com/awardweb/hugos/index.shtml

Lambda Literary Award (Gay and Lesbian only)
http://www.lambdalit.org/lammy/index.htm

Minnesota Book Awards (Minnesota authors only)
http://www.mnbooks.org/cfb/awards.htm

The Mythopoeic Awards
http://www.mythsoc.org/awards.html

Prometheus Award (info only)
http://www.lfs.org/PROMETHE.HTM

Sandeen and Sullivan Award
http://www.undpress.nd.edu/undpsansull.htm

Saphire Awards
http://members.aol.com/sfreditor/bestsfr.htm

Sidewise Award (Alternative History)
http://www.uchronia.net/sidewise/

Spectrum Awards (gay and lesbian sci-fi)
http://www.lambdasf.org/spectrum/

Bram Stoker Awards
http://www.horror.org/stoker.htm

James Tiptree Jr. Award
http://www.tiptree.org/index.html

The Australian Vogel Award
http://ncc1701.apana.org.au/~larrik...es/ozvogel.html

Whitbread Award (British Authors)
http://www.whitbread-bookawards.co.uk/

National Book Awards
http://www.publishersweekly.com/nbf/docs/winners5.html

British Fantasy Society Awards
http://www.herebedragons.co.uk/bfs/awards99.htm

Nebula Awards
http://www.sfwa.org/awards/

Eppie Awards
http://www.eclectics.com/epic/

Dream Realm Awards
http://www.dream-realm-awards.com

Frankfurt E-book Award
http://www.frankfurt-ebook-awards.org/

Pearl Award
http://www.writerspace.com/ParanormalRomance/

Award Winners and Notable Books
http://books.rpmdp.com/awards/awards.htm

Ambassador Book Awards
http://www.bookweb.org/home/news/btw/1965.html

Kirriyama Pacific Rim Book Award
http://pacificrimvoices.org/

Robert F. Kennedy Book Award
http://www.rfkmemorial.org/book_award.htm

Governor General's Literary Awards (Canadian writers)
http://www.canadacouncil.ca/news/pr...es/co9937-e.asp

The Giller Prize (Canadian writers only $25,000 prize)
http://www.thegillerprize.org/

Commonwealth Writers Prize
http://www.booktrust.org.uk/

The Bakeless Literary Prize
http://www.middlebury.edu/~blwc/

The Charlotte Zolotow Award (best children's picture book)
http://144.92.171.181/ccbc/zolotow.htm

Show Me Readers Award (children's books grade 1-3)
http://tiger.coe.missouri.edu/~masl/awards/showme.html

Mark Twain Award (children's books grade 4+)
http://tiger.coe.missouri.edu/~masl/awards/marktw.html

Dorothy Canfield Children's Book Award
http://www.mps.k12.vt.us/msms/dcf/dcf.html

The Rysling Award (poetry)
http://home.earthlink.net/~dragontea/rhys.html

http://www.bookwire.com/bookwire/ot...ook-Awards.html

http://www.literature-awards.com/bookawards.htm

The Indie 100 book promotion contest
http://www.razorpages.com

Writing Articles

When we discussed linking, I mentioned the tactic of writing articles. Articles are one of the best ways to promote your book and to set yourself up as an expert in your field. This tactic works exceptionally well for non-fiction, business type books, but no matter what your book is about, you need to write and submit articles.

The basic concept behind submitting articles is that people will find your article and click to your blog site or website. In addition, many bloggers will put your article on their blogs giving you more exposure, more traffic and more links. In addition, when you write and submit articles, you are providing a valuable service. Writing genuine articles requires you to share a part of your expertise with the world and people will appreciate your willingness to share what you know.

There are literally thousands of sites you can submit your articles to, but the most common approach is to post your articles on the top 100 sites and let the other services download your article from these top 100. While you can submit articles yourself, you can also use article submission services to help you.

The following sites accept free articles for publication:

http://www.ezinearticles.com
http://www.ideamarketers.com
http://www.marketing-seek.com
http://www.certificate.net
http://www.web-source.net
http://www.theukmarketer.com
http://www.MakingProfit.com/articles
http://w.moreover.com/site/publishers/index.html

Google Books

One day I wanted to find some information about Steven Covey's, "The 7 Habits of Highly Successful People." I went to the Google search bar and typed in the title to his book. I figured I would be taken directly to his website, but instead, I ended up on his Google book page. To view the same site I found, type in this address:

http://books.google.combooks?ct=result&psp=1&id=q5JFe NF196EC&dq=the+seven+habits+of+highly+effective+ people&q=the+seven+habits+of+highly+effective+people&pgis=1

Here is an explanation of the Google Book Search for people (hopefully your future readers) looking for books. This is reprinted from Google's site:

What is Google Book Search?

Search the full text of books to find ones that interest you and learn where to buy or borrow them.

How does Google Book Search work?

Book Search works just like web search: Try a search on Google Book Search or on Google.com. When we find a book whose content contains a match for your search terms, we'll link to it in your search results. Clicking on a book result, you'll be able to see everything from a few short excerpts to the entire book, depending on a few different factors.

What can I view?

Each book includes an 'About This Book' page with basic bibliographic data like title, author, publication date, length and subject. For some books you may also see additional information like key terms and phrases, references to the book from scholarly publications or other books, chapter titles and a list of related books. For every book, you'll see links directing you to bookstores where you can buy the book and libraries where you can borrow it.

Full view: If we've determined that a book is out of copyright, or the publisher or rightsholder has given us permission, you'll be able to page through the entire book from start to finish, as many times as you like. If the book is in the public domain, you'll also be able download, save and print a PDF version to read at your own pace.

Limited preview: If a publisher or author has joined our Partner Program, you'll be able to see a few full pages from the book as a preview. You can conduct multiple searches within the book, or browse through the available pages (there's a limit to the amount of the book you can view online).

Snippet view: Clicking on the book result, you'll be taken to the 'About this book' page. If you choose to search within the book, for each search term we'll display up to three snippets of text from the book, showing your search term in context. You can enter additional searches to help you decide whether you've found the right book. As always in Book Search, you'll see links to places where you can buy or borrow the book.

No preview available: For books where we're unable to show you snippets, you'll see an 'About This Book' page displaying bibliographic information about the book, plus links to help you find it in a bookstore or library.

This explanation on how Google Book Search can help people find books shows you the value Google can bring to you as an author. Since Google accounts for over 60% of total searches, having your book in an easy to find search function is a great tool. To set up your book, simply go to https://books.google.com/partner/ and follow the instructions.

Summary

I honestly think I could write a book longer than *War and Peace* if I tried to list every online tactic available to us and how to use them. I see little value in making the attempt as these tactics tend to change quickly. In addition, the best way to learn how to use internet tools is to simply begin using them. That's why I like the concept of fast and furious. My experience has taught me the value of learning new online tactics quickly and then implementing them as furiously as possible.

8

Leverage Your Tactics

• • •

*Curly: One thing. Just one thing: You stick to that
and the rest don't mean [nothin']*
***Mitch:** But, what is the "one thing?"*
Curly: [smiles] That's what *you* have to find out.

The above dialogue is from the movie City Slickers. Mitch Robbins (played by Billy Crystal) is trying to figure out the essence of life, love and how to be happy. Curly (played by Jack Palance) is a no-nonsense cowboy and tells him simply that he has to find the "One" thing. Finding the "One" thing sounds simple and yet very few people ever discover their one thing.

The "One" thing for a book to sell well is that it must generate Word of Mouth or WOM for short. That's all you have to do. Sounds simple, and yet very few authors ever achieve this ever elusive goal. If you analyze every promotional tactic discussed in this book, you'll see that the purpose of each tactic is to create word of mouth. Ever wonder why every author wants to get on Oprah? Because she's the biggest WOM in the market. Look at the brief list of tactics you can use to promote your book:

- Podcasting

- Book Trailers

- Book signings

- Websites

- Blogging

- Book Reviews

- Book Giveaways

- Press Releases

- TV interviews

- Radio interviews

- Newspaper interviews

The purpose of every one of these tactics is to create Word of Mouth. *The Da Vinci Code* is, of course, a huge success, but I didn't read *The Da Vinci Code* until a good friend of mine said he had read it and that he thought it was very provocative. Just about every book I've ever read has been the direct result of Word of Mouth.

Malcolm Gladwell wrote a book called *The Tipping Point* (www.gladwell.com). Gladwell talks about connectors and mavens and salespeople and he discusses terms like epidemic and contagious and "stickiness." When you get to the very end of *The Tipping Point*, the author concludes by discussing that what causes a tipping point is word of mouth. That's it. Figuring out how to create WOM for a book is the "One" thing every author needs to figure out.

In order to create WOM for your book requires you, the author (with help from your agent or publisher if you are not self-publishing), to "invent your strategy." Everything you do will affect your ability to create WOM. Is your title "sticky?" Did you write a timely book or a book that is of interest to a great many people? Did you write a book that is exceptionally funny or revolutionary? Does your cover create interest? When you talk about your book, are you highlighting the points that will create WOM?

We were working with an author who had written his first novel and he had decided to self-publish. Self-publishing a work of fiction is a difficult task. This author was very active in self-promoting his book and was holding book readings every few weeks. He and I went to lunch one day and he said he was frustrated that his book readings weren't generating book sales. I had read his book and so I asked him which parts he was reading from. After he told me, I said that I didn't think the parts he was reading were the most interesting parts of his story. He was choosing his reading sections based on the logical flow of his story, i.e. beginning, middle, end, and also on parts he felt were highly insightful. He wasn't thinking of which parts were the most *interesting* though. When you focus on the goal of creating word of mouth, you will highlight the parts of your book that are interesting to your readers.

The second point is that whether or not your book catches the WOM fire is partially due to serendipity. Besides being a naturally controversial book (saying that the holy grail was the offspring of Christ), the Da Vinci Code hit bookshelves during the George W. Bush presidency. A major reason Mr. Bush was elected was the strength of the red states. An evangelical firestorm was broiling in the US creating a polarization effect separating the "liberals" from the "good guys". Many conservatives found the allegations in Dan Brown's work of "fiction" preposterous and an affront to their beliefs. The book generated a lot of buzz, both positive and negative.

Dan Brown's book would have been a best seller without the underlying political sentiments going on at the time it was published. Dan Brown is a well-known author and he had written a best-seller type of novel. But the fact that his book sold over 40 million copies was a fact of fate—it was serendipitous.

Another great example is Harriet Stowe's book *Uncle Tom's Cabin*. She wrote her book about 10 years before the civil war started. Her book was the best selling book when it came out, second only to the Holy Bible. She sold 300,000 copies in the first year. When Abraham Lincoln met Mrs. Stowe in the white house, he said, "This is the little woman who started a war." Uncle Tom's Cabin is said to have had an impact on the outcome of the war as her book created such anti-slavery sentiment in England that while the UK wanted to protect its interest in the cotton trade of the South, it simply couldn't go to the aid of the South because it feared its citizens would reject such action. If Mrs. Stowe had written her book a hundred years earlier or a hundred years later, Uncle Tom's Cabin may have died a slow death on the desk of some New York Publisher.

These two examples, *The Da Vinci Code* and *Uncle Tom's Cabin*, do not say that in order to have a best seller you have to hit the timing just right. But they do point out the role that timing and serendipity play in a book's success. The point is that even if an author writes an excellent book, whether that book becomes a national bestseller is up to many variables. The tools an author uses can help an author get the word out about his or her book, but whether the book sells 1,000 copies or 1,000,000 copies is dependant on many factors.

I hope you're not discouraged by this discussion of serendipity. Understanding the law of serendipity is vital to your success and enjoyment as an author and especially as a self-publishing author. In Chapter 2 we talked about setting a reasonable goal for your book. I like the goal of selling 2,500 because this goal is reasonable for many authors. If you plan to sell 2,500 copies and build your plan accordingly, your overall risk will be minimized but you still give your book a good chance of catching the WOM fire.

If you strategically leverage the tools in this book, you are prudently going about catching a wave that might cause your book to explode. If it doesn't catch that wave, well, you're not going to go bankrupt and you've had an incredible experience.

If I had a dollar for every author in the world who believes his or her book is the next best seller, I'd be a rich man. Let's assume there are 4 million people with books ready to print right now. The reality is that the market cannot support 4 million best sellers. Currently, mainstream publishers publish only 175,000 titles and only a handful of those published books are going to make it to the New York Times bestseller list.

Does this mean that your book in not good? No. Does this mean that people will not find value in your book? No. What this means is that you need to focus on your niche market. You need to find the few thousand people who need the message in your book and if you can successfully sell to those few thousand people and make a profit, then you are a successful author.

By putting forth your best efforts to find your readers, you may "hit it big." But your goal should be to make your book selling efforts a profitable venture and I propose that just about any author can achieve this goal. It might be that the book you are currently working on is a stepping-stone to a bigger project, a book that will sell hundreds of thousand of copies.

Leveraging your tactics is about creating a plan to achieve a reasonable goal. The remainder of this chapter is a real business plan created for Diana Derval, the author I introduced in Chapter Two. Diana first published her book in French and after selling several thousand copies decided to translate her book into English. Diana and I met during the pre-launch of Authors On The Net and so she and I began working together to create a real-life case study based on the DRILL concepts. I track the progress of Diana's self-publishing efforts on my blog, www.howtopublishabookblog.com and you can read more about Diana, her book and her workshops by going to www.wait-marketing.com.

The plan you see reprinted here is a simple plan because authors are better off with a simple plan rather than a complicated plan as long as the plan has the essential elements. The success of your plan depends on how well you execute the plan. Straightforward, easy to implement plans have a higher chance of success.

The Diana Derval Case Study—a complete look at the DRILL system in action
Developing Realistic Goals for Diana's Book

Goals
When I asked Diana what her goals were, here is what she told me:

- To become recognized world-wide as a Marketing Guru

- To sell **100,000** books

- To have my book picked up by a mainstream publisher

- To close more seminar business and speaking engagements

We then began to analyze her goals. A goal, by most business definitions, is something that can be measured. With that in mind, her first goal, "To become recognized **worldwide** as a Marketing Guru," is more of an overall objective or vision than a measurable goal. But we decided to leave this goal in place. We can do that since we are *inventing* our own plan and I'm not sure defining this goal more specifically will add any value. For example, we could say that the goal is to be interviewed by CNBC 10 times, be asked for advice by the Wall Street Journal 20 times and so forth. There are many ways to quantify Diana's goal of becoming known worldwide as a Marketing Guru. Since one way for her to measure this goal is to sell **100,000** books, we decided to focus on that goal.

Diana's goal of selling 100,000 books is a great goal, but we decided we needed an interim goal of selling 2,500 copies in six months to help us make decisions on how best to utilize her resources. Many authors have goals like, to become a best seller or to sell as many books as possible. These two statements are not measurable goals. A goal to become a best selling author is more like a vision statement. Having a reasonable number written down and staring you in the face is an important first step to selling books.

To sell 100,000 books (or more), Diana will most likely need to be picked up by a traditional publisher or be prepared to spend tens of thousands of dollars. Diana does not have that kind of money to invest in a project as risky as selling books.

The realistic number Diana decided to put for her second goal is 2,500 copies. This number accomplishes three things:

1. A plan to sell **2,500** books will fit her budget and risk level. I put risk level here because how much money Diana has in her bank account shouldn't be the only factor that drives her investment decision. How she values risk is the more important factor. If she has $50,000 in the bank and feels that dumping all that money into promoting her book in order to sell 100,000 copies and she's okay with that kind of risk-taking, then she might choose to go that route. I, as her coach, would strongly disagree, as I believe in a prudent investment strategy. My prudent investment strategy was developed because I've seen too many authors spend thousands on ads in magazines and on large print runs only to watch their money turn to vapor before their eyes.

2. A plan to sell 2,500 books will help Diana get picked up by a traditional publisher, her third goal. The experts disagree on this "magic" number, but just about all experts agree that once an author demonstrates the ability to sell a good number of books on their own, a publisher begins to show interest. Whether that number is 2,500, 5,000 or 10,000 doesn't matter. If Diana can go to Random House and show them she's sold 2,500 copies, she will have a much better chance of selling her book. More likely, Random House will be calling her.

3. Selling 2,500 books gives Diana cash flow and credibility. If she sells 2,500 books for $20.00 a book she'll earn $50,000 gross and if we assume she nets 30% after printing and marketing costs,

she'll make $15,000. She won't get rich this way, but as she plans to write more books, this cash flow can be used to either keep promoting *Wait Marketing* or be used on a new book.

Diana's third goal, "To be picked up by a main-stream publisher," is a good goal. She can measure it since we'll know when a mainstream publisher picks up her book. However, just getting picked up by a publisher is a little vague and dangerous. We want to be in such a good position that the best publisher for a business book like Diana's will contract with her. There are a lot of small publishers in the market and some of these publishers, even if they are ethical, may not have the resources to sell Diana's book effectively. I don't think Diana means she wants to get picked up by a publisher running an office out of her home. She wants a Random House or a Double-day or a Scribner.

Diana's fourth goal is also not defined well enough. She needs to put a number of closed clients. In the beginning, two closed clients a month would be ambitious, but in six months' time Diana thinks she can handle four new clients a month. We'll start with two a month. We'll also create a fifth goal for her speaking engagements and start by trying to close two engagements each month.

Diana's goals now look like this:

1. To become recognized world-wide as a Market-ing Guru

2. To sell 2,500 copies 6 months from the launch date (June 15th)

3. To have my book picked up by a major publisher in my field, i.e. Scribner

4. To close 2 seminar clients each month

5. To close 2 speaking engagements each month

Except for the first goal, all of Diana's goals can be measured. These goals will be used to drive the rest of her plan.

The goals each author develops will be different, but each author should follow this process and come up with some good, measurable goals. Having a coach to help refine your goals is a good idea. Your coach can be a respected friend, a spouse or a paid consultant. Another point to keep in mind is the concept of phases. We'll talk about Phases when we get to the strategy section, but first, let's identify Diana's target audience.

Researching Diana's target audience

For most products and services, wide ranges of people are potential buyers. But since marketing dollars are scarce, most companies choose one or a few of their best target customers to zero in on. Authors need to do the same. When I started ZDocs, I told people I printed anything. After struggling for two years, I changed my focus and said we specialize in printing books. My business has been growing 60% year-on-year since making this decision. And while our marketing focus is on books, we still get requests for brochures, postcards, wedding invitations and other products.

In Chapter 2, we identified Diana's market as large corporations with multiple operating units. We plan to focus on companies like Starbucks, FedEx Kinko's, Limited Brands, etc. Please refer back to Chapter 2 to review how we developed this target audience.

When Diana and I began our discussions, our target audience was defined as Entrepreneurs. On the surface, this target audience sounded well defined, but by drilling further, we developed a much clearer picture of the customer we should focus on. Two weeks after defining our audience, Diana sent me her plan of attack.

Diana contacted a marketing firm and discussed her target audience. The marketing firm devised a tactic to put 50 gift packages together. Inside the gift package was a signed copy of her book, some French cookies and a letter. The letter was written specifically to each company with wait marketing ideas that the company can implement.

Writing these kind of specific letters will take about a month. That's a lot of time to get the word out to her 50 target customers. But if only one of these companies invites Diana to come speak to them, the payoff might be tens of thousands of dollars in sold books, seminars and keynote speeches. The effort is worth the potential payoff.

In addition, Diana knows that if one company buys her product, that experience will create word of mouth and help her get into other companies. The ultimate payoff could be hundreds of thousands of dollars.

On a smaller note, Diana wanted to offer her potential customers the opportunity to download a PDF chapter of her book, a common practice these days. She asked me what chapter she should give away. I immediately told her Chapter 5 because Chapter 5 is when the "action" begins. In Chapter 5, Diana begins to show entrepreneurs how to implement her concepts and as an entrepreneur, this is the Chapter that got my attention.

Diana instantly agreed with me, but she said her publisher in France thought that giving Chapter 5 away would be giving too much valuable information for free. But her publisher in France wasn't working with the same target audience we were working with.

Deciding what chapter to give away for free is a small decision, but authors often get hung up on these kinds of decisions. With a target audience decided, making decisions becomes easier. I get at least one phone call a week by someone wanting to sell me something, like an ad in a magazine or a piece of equipment. I used to listen to all the sales people thinking they might have something to help my business. But after I decided on my target audience, I can now decide on the spot if the sales person has a product or service that I might want.

What if Diana and I hadn't taken the time to define a clear target audience? Let's say we just stuck with our "all entrepreneurs" audience. Our approach would be different, as we cannot send out gift packages to every entrepreneur in the United States. Here are some ideas our plan might include if we were going after all entrepreneurs:

- Attend small business conferences

- Seek speaking engagements at small business conferences

- Promote book on entrepreneur websites/social networks

- Advertise in trade magazines

- All the other tactics discussed in this book like virtual book tours

The tactics listed above are great tactics and Diana will be using them in her real plan even though she is focused on large corporations with multiple units. The difference, however, is that if she had not defined her target audience with the large corporations in mind, she would not have developed the gift box idea.

While Diana will be happy to sell her book to anyone, she will attain greater success if she can close a deal with a company like Starbucks. Every business I know seems to follow two basic rules. One rule is the 80/20 rule. This rule states that 80% of a company's revenues comes from 20% of its customers. The second rule is that you will spend just as much effort earning $100,000 as you will spend earning $10,000. For example, I've spent a month closing a large corporate customer and I've also spent a month closing a $1,500 order from an independent author. To close both deals required me to produce several bids, make several phone calls and so forth. The effort spent was nearly equal but the end payout was vastly different.

Diana's book is a business book and in many ways she has an easier time defining her target audience. But fiction writers define their audiences too. Stephen King writes for people who like horror stories. Tom Clancy and John Grisham also have their audiences.

For authors with a work of fiction, my first recommendation is to expend all efforts on selling their book to a mainstream publisher. These authors will need the publisher's expertise and ability to get into the proper channels. Selling a manuscript to a publisher, however, still requires authors to research their target audience. Your target audience when looking for a publisher for your book are those publishers who work with the genre of fiction your book fits into.

The average time it takes to find a publisher is 18 months and will result in many rejection letters. Publishers will reject your book for many reasons. Your query might not be written correctly, your book might not fit their niche, the publisher may currently have too many projects on their docket, you might be an "unknown" author, and so forth. My guess is that most books do not get rejected because the book itself is "bad," although that is certainly one reason your book might be rejected.

If you are committed to drilling until you find your treasure and you have chosen to get published rather than to self-publish, then go about the process just as strategically as you would if you were self-publishing. You might focus on selling 2,500 books and promoting yourself using the tactics discussed in this book, or you might spend 18 months scouring the world for a publisher to take a chance with you. Or you might use both approaches simultaneously. Getting published is a worthwhile goal and although it may take several years and several books until you *get published*, the treasure will be extremely satisfying.

DRILL is about promoting books, not writing books, but when it comes to selling fiction, good writing is one of the key success factors and good writing is a blend of talent and practice. Another key success factor is having ideas and publishers like authors who have many ideas for stories. A third key success factor for becoming a published writer is writing what the market wants. Ever wonder why every year hundreds of magazine articles and books are published about losing weight? People buy magazines and books about losing weight. People like to be scared so horror books sell well. People like action, so they buy Tom Clancy and John Grisham.

The question I'm addressing here is, do you want to publish your *book* or do you want to become a published *author*? If you want to become a published author, your strategy should be built around this goal. Tactics would include writing short stories for magazines, entering writing contests, attending writer's conferences, sending query letters off selling your story idea *before* you spend the next two years writing your story and using the tactics in *DRILL* to promote your books until you get picked up by the big guys.

Inventing a Strategy for Diana's book

In Chapter 3 we defined that strategy is: *a plan, method, or series of maneuvers or stratagems for obtaining a specific goal or result: a strategy for getting ahead in the world. Armed with measurable goals and a clear idea of the target audience for Diana's book, we can now invent her strategy.*

When thinking about strategy, it is easy to get sucked into tactics, but as we discussed in chapter 3, strategy is the bridge between our goals and our tactics. The reason we need a strategy is to effectively implement our tactics. A strategy for war would entail where to position troops, when to end diplomatic discussions, what kind of troops needed to win a battle and so forth. Tactics are employed once the battle begins.

As Diana's overall goal for herself is to become a world-renowned marketing guru, the strategy we create will be a bridge between the tactics we use and reaching this goal. Diana's strategy is as follows:

1. Position herself as an expert

2. Focus on key markets, Europe, North America, Asia

3. Align herself with key people

4. Allocate the necessary resources

5. Create a timeline

Regarding point (1), Diana has spent much of her life studying marketing. She has an MBA in marketing and is a professor at a major University. More importantly, Diana has researched a new topic in the field of marketing and she has coined the term "Wait Marketing." Diana has turned her research into an easy-to-understand book called "Wait Marketing," an important step in her pursuit to become a marketing guru.

Now that she has positioned herself, Diana is ready to take her message to the world. Her strategy is to focus on key markets. Her Phase I strategy is to launch her book and her workshops in French-speaking markets. This market was chosen primarily because of proximity and familiarity. French is Diana's native language and France and other French speaking countries are major industrialized countries. Diana knows she can use the credibility she will gain in France and other French speaking countries to propel her message to other countries.

After her French launch, Diana will publish her book in English, the most widely spoken language on the planet and the language of the largest market in the world, the United States. Launching her book in the US is part of her Phase II strategy. Rather than rolling her book out in major cities, Diana's strategy will be to focus on large, innovative companies with hundreds or thousands of smaller operating units located nationwide. Phase III will be to translate her book in other languages such as Japanese and Chinese and to begin selling her book in Asia.

To accomplish her goals, Diana will need to align herself with the right people. She will need to find people who can help her get the attention of decision makers inside the large companies she is targeting. She will need to align herself with people who can help find her speaking and seminar engagements.

Diana has a big, ambitious vision and to implement the tactics she has chosen will cost money. Diana can go several routes. She can deplete her savings account. She can apply for every credit card sent to her in the mail, she can find sponsors or she can start out small, build cash flows and use the cash flows to grow her business. How much money she'll need to invest up-front depends largely on her timeline.

Diana wants to move aggressively and in order to minimize her upfront investment, she'll need to work strategically. At the time of this writing, Diana's French launch is complete and has generated a small amount of cash flow. She will use this cash flow to translate, edit and print her book in English. Her budget to launch the book in the US is $10,000 US.

Creating a strategy is the most difficult part of the DRILL system. Goals are fairly easy to identify and so is a target audience. Tactics are like toy blocks lying around on the floor just waiting to be organized into recognizable shapes, say a house for example. Strategy is the act of thinking about the most efficient way to get the blocks organized into the shape you want.

Each part of Diana's strategy has significant implications. For example, if she were trying to become a world-renowned marketing guru without her academic credentials, she would be fighting an uphill battle. While laymen might believe her, experts most likely would not and she needs the experts to help make her a guru.

Diana could have chosen to enter the US market first, but focusing on her local market is, in my opinion, a smart move. By starting out in her local market, she can get publicity, she can build relationships, and she can work with local companies to make case studies and so forth. Starting local and then expanding is often a good way to begin, even for authors not trying to cross international borders.

Moving beyond your local market is usually a Phase II maneuver. An author can expand to the top 10 book selling cities in the US or other sales channels where the author's book has the best chance of selling, like boat Marinas for books about how to sail. Thinking strategically can significantly help to reduce losses and improve a book's chances for survival.

Choosing whom to align yourself with is another strategic decision. Diana needs to identify the people who can help get her book in the right hands. These people may be publishers or consultants or marketing professionals. With this strategy in place, Diana will begin to look for trade organizations and other places to approach.

Diana may have the best book in the world and a great strategy to sell it, but without resources to implement her tactics, her book will have a hard time getting off the ground. We had an author who identified a new market for his book—young college students. Once the author found this audience, he decided to approach Coca Cola to sponsor a print run of 100,000 books. This author's innovative idea was the direct result of knowing his audience. Once he knew who to sell to, he invented his own strategy to sell to his audience. I doubt any book-selling consultant could have come up with a better idea than approaching Coca Cola to print up 100,000 books.

Laying out the tactics for promoting Diana's book

This is the section where we look at all the tactics available to use and choose which tactics will deliver the best return. Here is Diana's list of online tactics she has chosen:

Online tactics

1. Blogsite. Diana's blog can be found by clicking on www.wait-marketing.com. Diana uses her blog as her marketing centerpiece.

2. Get her English book reviewed

3. Begin writing articles to post in hundreds of eZines

4. Run press releases on PR Web and other online sources

5. Get her book on every available online bookstore, i.e. Amazon

6. Start a book club on Google and Yahoo

7. Run an email campaign, beginning with Diana's own inner-circle

8. Expand her email campaign to include partners

9. Set up her Google Book account

10. Begin to social network

11. Hold a webinar

12. Put a flash banner on relevant websites

13. Hold monthly tele-seminars

14. Create a virtual book tour

We want to start with the online tactics for three reasons: 1. they are relatively inexpensive, 2. customers need to be able to find her book online in as many places as possible and 3. in France, Diana is having more success selling online than in bookstores.

Off-line tactics

1. Send gift boxes out to 50 target companies

2. Set up interviews with local and national media and with trade journals

3. Set up a 10 day speaking tour/book signing tour

Our offline tactic list is much shorter because the time it takes to implement just these three offline tactics will require more time and possibly more money than her online tactics. Speaking/Book tours can be quite expensive and not too productive so that will be one of the last actions we take. However, we know that a good speaking/book tour may also create a tipping point so we want to try at least one tour. But the tour needs to come after some online momentum has been developed and if Diana can close one major account, then her speaking/book tour has a better chance to succeed.

Once all the online tactics are put in place, we will begin attacking our target audience. The two primary activities we'll invest our time in are getting interviewed in various media and sending proposals directly to selected companies. While getting interviewed in the Wall Street Journal or the New York Times would be wonderful, our push will be to get interviewed in trade journals, on business-related radio shows and on business-related TV shows.

The most exciting tactic we will employ is to send customized proposals—the gift boxes—to 50 targeted companies. Again, having just one company embrace Diana's concepts will be a huge success: in terms of book sales, seminars, key note speeches and referrals.

To be successful, we know we need to get creative. Some other ideas we are exploring are:

- Host a webinar and put the recording on a CD. Then send the CD to key decision makers inside our targeted customers. We will also send an email to these people with the audio clip included.

- Introduce the idea to these customers of holding an internal competition. In this competition, each business unit competes using the concepts of Wait Marketing.

Whether these ideas work or not is extremely important for Diana, but for the reader of this book, the important message is to see the process we are going through. If you go back to the introduction where we discussed the author's mindset, one of the attributes of an author is that he or she is innovative. The ideas Diana is coming up with are not ideas she read about in a book or heard about from her friends. Her ideas are the result of her own brainstorming.

I've worked with many authors and one truism, for me anyway, is that authors do not want to be told what they should do. Authors are fiercely independent people, like entrepreneurs, and they will either figure out how to be successful or go down in a blaze of glory. When an author combines ambition, talent and ideas with a well-defined plan, the author creates amazing possibilities for his or her book.

Leveraging Diana's Assets

The plan we have just presented is an example of how an author leverages his or her assets. Your plan ties everything together. Your plan crystallizes your thinking. Every so-called expert on book publishing and book promoting will tell you that you need a plan. Likewise, the *DRILL* system is all about building your plan.

Despite the general consensus that all authors (and all businesses for that matter) need to have a plan, few people actually develop one, or if they do, the plan is not executed correctly. The purpose of including a real author's plan in this book is to illustrate the value of a well thought-out plan.

Without going through our planning process, Diana would not have identified exactly the kind of companies she wanted to sell to. The ideas were in her head, but the ideas were not developed. Most authors have a sense of who their readers are and how they might find them and convince them to buy their book, but without a plan the author generally flounders around, wasting time and money and producing few actual book sells.

In addition, the planning process Diana went through generated some clever and original ideas. I am very wary of someone selling a "guaranteed" system for selling books or a "guaranteed" way of getting to the number one spot on Amazon or a "guaranteed" way of getting on Oprah. Books are just too diverse to fit any one system. No major publisher can guarantee a book's success. The closest thing to a guarantee for a book's success is a book written by an already best-selling author, like Stephen King. He's a pretty good bet. But when Stephen King's publisher took a chance on Mr. King's first book, *Carrie*, no one could have predicted that the book would launch one of the most successful writing careers in history. I'll say it again, be wary of a guaranteed program for selling books.

The secret is that every author needs to find his or her own way, in other words, every authors needs to invent his or her own strategy. Once goals are developed, target audiences researched and strategies invented, the author can choose which tactics to use and how to use them in the most efficient way possible.

Leverage everything with your Blog

The final point in this chapter about leveraging your assets is to link every possible selling tactic to your blog. Every activity listed in Diana's plan can be linked to Diana's blog. Let's see how that would look:

1. Get her English book reviewed

    a. Diana will make a post on her blog that her book has been reviewed

    b. Diana will post the actual review on her blog

2. Begin writing articles to post in hundreds of eZines

    a. Every eZine article will track back to Diana's blog

    b. Diana will put her articles on her blog which helps her SEO

3. Run press releases on PR Web and other online sources

    a. Each press release will track back to her blog

    b. Diana will post the press releases on her blog

4. Get her book on every available online bookstore, i.e. Amazon

    a. Amazon puts author websites/blog sites on their sales pages

    b. If a reader finds Diana's book on Amazon and sees the link to her blog, the reader can click over and learn more about Diana and her book(s).

5. Start a book club on Google and Yahoo

    a. The book clubs will link to Diana's blog

    b. Diana can post interesting ideas from the book clubs on her blog

6. Run an email campaign, beginning with Diana's own inner-circle

    a. Diana will collect email addresses on her blog

    b. Diana include these opted-in email addresses to sell books

7. Set up her Google Book account

    a. People will find Diana's book when they search

    b. If interested, people will then click over to her blog

8. Begin to social network

    a. Blogging is all about social networking

    b. Diana will leave comments on other blogs tracking back to hers

    c. People will leave comments on her blog

9. Hold a webinar and monthly tele-seminars

    a. Diana will promote her webinar/tele-seminar on her blog

    b. People will sign up for her webinar/tele-seminar from her blog

    c. Diana will generate Podcasts from her webinars/tele-seminars and post these Podcasts on her blog

10. Create a Virtual Book Tour

    a. Diana will invite visitors to her blog to attend the VBT

    b. Diana will post the VBT on her blog for future visitors to listen to

11. Put a flash banner on relevant websites

    a. All banners will post on her blog

    b. When someone clicks on a banner on an affiliate website, the customer will be directed back to Diana's blog

12. Send proposal letters to 50 target companies

    a. The proposal letters will invite potential customers to visit her blog

    b. Diana will post about her plan to sell to large, multi-unit companies

13. Set up interviews with local and national media and with trade journals

   a. Interviewers can use Diana's blog for background information.

   b. In addition, any interview, written or audio, will be posted on her blog

14. Develop a book signing tour

   a. Diana will post the schedule for her book signing tour

   b. Diana will make posts about what happened at her signings

Diana has a well-defined strategy and every activity she uses to sell her book will be tracked on her blog. She is making it convenient for customers to find her book and she is leveraging her ability to sell the greatest number of books.

Think of a customer, or reader, as a big whale. To catch a whale, you need to put a lot of hooks—harpoons—in it. I had heard of the Da Vinci code 10 times before I bought a copy. In other words, I had 10 harpoons in me before I finally gave in and bought Dan Brown's book. Effective advertising campaigns use a combination of flyers, billboards, radio ads and television ads. The more hooks in the whale you place, the more likely you are to catch it. The same is true for landing a reader. By leveraging all your tactics in a well-defined plan and by connecting all your activities to your blog, you will have a better chance of landing a customer.

Epilogue

• • •

*"Keep away from people who try to belittle your ambitions.
Small people always do that, but the really great make you
feel that you, too, can become great."*
— MARK TWAIN

Remember that guy in the prologue digging his hole to find his treasure? The story said that he "climbed a mountain to find his buried treasure." Why is it important to note that he climbed a mountain just to start digging a hole? The man's climbing the mountain is symbolic to an author writing a book. Climbing mountains is not easy and neither is writing a valuable book. But getting to the top of the mountain—or to the end of a book—is the point when the digging begins.

Continuing the metaphor, the man digging for treasure has done a lot of research pointing him to the mountain he is standing on. Likewise, an author has researched his target audience and has written a book that people will want to buy. If the man is on the wrong mountain, no amount of digging will lead him to his treasure. If an author has written a book with no audience in mind or has written a sloppy book, it will be difficult for the author to find his treasure.

DRILL is not intended to help people write good books for well-defined audiences. Many other experts have covered this topic extensively. The *DRILL* system is designed to help all authors—published and self-published—formulate a plan to promote their books in the most cost-effective way possible.

The tactics outlined in *DRILL* are by no means exhaustive. In fact, tactics may be as limitless as an author's imagination. My goal with *DRILL* was to introduce authors to some of the key online tactics available today. As I am a staunch believer that each author must invent his or her own strategy and then choose tactics to execute that strategy, writing a book that covers every tactic known to humankind was not my purpose.

Stephen King once said that ideas for stories are like millions of lights shining in his trees outside his house. If Stephen King lived to be 1,000 years old, I have no doubt that he would write 3,000 stories. Ideas for promoting books are like the shining lights Mr. King describes. The trick is choosing which ideas to implement. Deciding which ideas to implement is largely determined by what results an author is trying to achieve and what target audience an author is trying to serve.

Why do we sometimes start a project and then fail to see the project through to the end? Procrastination, distractions and fears are just a few reasons we may stop drilling before we find our treasure. Mark Twain, in his quote above, points out another reason. People who may discourage us from pursuing our ambitions surround us all. The founder of FedEx did not get a particularly good grade on his paper he wrote while attending Yale. But every time I have to ship something that must be delivered on time, I'm grateful Mr. Fred Smith didn't let the negative review by his professor keep him from pursuing his vision.

My goal in writing this book is to help authors keep drilling until they reach their treasure. Some authors may find their treasure rather easily, but for others it may take years. Some authors may need to write 10 books before they find their treasure and other authors may hit pay dirt with their first book.

What excites me about life is that every human being has a story inside him or her. The story may be about ants living in the Sahara or how babies communicate through babbling nonsense or some other book with a small target audience. The good news for these types of authors and for all authors is they have tools available to them to help them reach their target audience. Not every author will be a best seller, but what if every author could sell enough copies to make a little profit? Now that's a paradigm shift.

DRILL is about working fast and furious and sticking with your project until you have accomplished your goals. *DRILL* gives authors a strategy to follow along with some of the key online tactics authors can use today. Once you begin using online tools like your own blog site, you will discover how fast you can take an idea out of your head and put it to work; like I did when I changed our Google ads at ZDocs. The speed at which you can take action is dizzying. But keep in mind that success takes time. Success takes effort. Keep drilling until you find your treasure because your treasure is out there waiting to be found.